If You Can't Tell It, Let Me Tell It!

"To God be the Glory for My Story"

by

Devetta Arnold

authorHOUSE

1663 LIBERTY DRIVE, SUITE 200
BLOOMINGTON, INDIANA 47403
(800) 839-8640
www.authorhouse.com

First published by AuthorHouse 07/29/04

ISBN: 1-4184-7972-1 (sc)

Printed in the United States of America
Bloomington, Indiana

This book is printed on acid-free paper.

Unless otherwise indicated, all Scripture quotations
are taken from the King James Version of the Bible

This Book Is Dedicated To All Women, Past, Present, and Future

This book is dedicated to women all over the world. This book is dedicated to all the women who were taught to be meek, lowly, and humble. This book is dedicated to all the women who were taught to be good girls, nice young ladies, strong women, submissive wives, and loving mothers. This book is dedicated to all the women who have been told that they would never amount to anything in life. This book is dedicated to women all over the world who have been belittled, abused, betrayed, and dismayed.

This book is dedicated to women all over the world who have been left alone, brokenhearted, grief-stricken, and in despair. This book is dedicated to women all over the world who have been socially rejected because of stereotyping. This book is dedicated to women all over the world who feel bound with bills, caring for their children with no support, while men seem to be free from that responsibility.

Women all over the world, as you read this book I pray that you find comfort in knowing that you are not alone. I pray that as you read this book the yokes of bondage, hurt, bitterness, pain, unforgiveness, and fear are broken from your mind, body, and spirit. I pray that as you are freed from the yokes of bondage, your eyes are opened and you begin to see yourself as the Woman of God he has predestined you to be. I pray the peace of God and peace with God, allows you to rest in God. I pray that each and every one of you know that there is nothing that you've done in your past that Jesus will not forgive you for. I pray that you know that there is nothing the blood of Jesus will not cleanse you of and the Holy Spirit deliver you from. I pray that you are empowered by the Holy Spirit. I pray that the Holy Spirit teaches as he guides you in all manner of truth. I pray that you are comforted in your times of loneliness. I pray that God heals your broken hearts and binds up the wounds according to his word. I pray that you are strengthened from within by the word of God being manifested in your life. I pray this prayer for you in the name of Jesus Christ. I pray in the name of Jesus because there is power in his name. I pray the name of Christ because of his character and he can not lie. To God be the Glory for you and your stories.

ACKNOWLEDGEMENT

All Glory be to God who is my father,
Jesus who is my Savior,
and the Holy Spirit who comforts and teaches me.

SPECIAL THANKS

An Awesome Woman Of God and Friend, Lisa Duckworth

CONTENTS

INTRODUCTION

In the past couple of years, I've experienced some things not as a young black woman, but as a woman. A woman who once believed that you could believe what a person said when they said it. I was raised and taught that your word was your bond. Life has taught me that everyone didn't raise their children. Some people let their children just grow up. I compare it to the sons of God and the sons of man philosophy, (but that's another book).

As a child, I was taught it was acceptable to love and give your heart to the "right person." However, I've learned that the "right person" takes on an entirely new meaning when the person becomes the "wrong person" for you. Now I know that just because a person acts like they are the "right person," talks like they are the "right person," doesn't mean they are the "right person" for me. It also doesn't mean they will do right by me or treat me like I should be treated as a human being.

As a child, I was called "tape recorder" because I told everything that happened around the house, at school, and yes, even at church. However funny the name may be now during my childhood, it was painful. It was a name that haunted me as I struggled to keep silent about things I heard, saw, experienced, and yes, sometimes even participated in. Keeping secrets, protecting others as well as myself is what I thought at the time. This is even what I was taught from time to time.

After years of growing up in the nice looking house on the outside full of hell on the inside, after the Ceremony that I thought was a marriage, after the Contractual Agreement that I thought was a marriage, after the physical, verbal abuse, sexual abuse, and domestic violence, I found that the secrets only kept me in bondage. The secrets kept me trapped in a world of abuse and a cycle of self destruction. The pain and drama continued year after year, relationship after relationship.

Painful experiences can make you feel like there's something wrong with you and you dare not tell anyone. Why tell anyone when it's so embarrassing? What will people think about you? You think that this can't be happening to anyone else but you. Sometimes you may even think you deserve it in some way. Now I know it was Satan's way of trying to stop me from fulfilling the plan God predestined for me.

In (Revelation 12:11), the word of God says "And they overcame him by the blood of the Lamb, and by the word of their testimony; and they loved not their lives unto the death." In order to have a testimony, you have to first testify. I've decided to be God's tape recorder. The more I learn how liberating his word is, the more I want to learn and share with others. In other words, you have to tell it. I will tell it. I will tell it over and over again and to God be the Glory for my story.

AUTHOR'S PREFACE

I've always heard about the trials and tribulation that women go through, but no one wants to tell their stories. Oftentimes, women are too embarrassed and/or humiliated to admit they are being abused or are suffering at the hands of others. Women continue to hurt because of the experiences they never talk about. They are either afraid and/or have been trained not to tell. I'm sure you've heard the saying, "Don't tell what goes on in this house" or "Don't tell any body your business." To a certain extent, that is true. But when it hides the abuse that goes on behind closed doors, it's just wrong.

I too was told not to talk about the abusive relationships I was in. I held the secrets in for years. As I held in the pain, I became hard hearted, bitter, and angry. When I did find the courage to tell my story, there was always someone who said I shouldn't mention it. I was told it wasn't a good idea to tell anyone because people will judge you. People will talk about you. People will think bad things about you. People will always throw your past in your face. I've found that no matter what you do, people have and will always talk about you.

For years, women all over the world have been hurt and wounded. Women have given their hearts, minds, and bodies for the sake of love or the lack thereof. I too have been one of these women not just once but several times. A friend described it to me like this. "You are a woman. Women love because it's just who God made them to be. When a woman gives her heart to a man, he can sell her a dream that will never come true. Not only will she buy this false dream, she'll also pay the price for it every time." I thought it was very profoundly stated. I too have been sold dreams in the past. The last one turned out to be a nightmare. The difference about this dream is this time I'm going to tell it. I'm not only telling it for me, I'm telling it so other women will know it's the only way to be free from the pain of the past.

Since the word of God says the truth shall set you free, tell the truth. If confession is good for the soul, why don't we talk about our pain and free ourselves? It's like being in church when the Servant of the Lord offers the opportunity for anyone to give their lives to Christ or come up for prayer. Many may want to come, but no one wants to be the first one to get up. As a Woman of God, I will no longer just exist. I am going to live the life Jesus said I could have, and have it more abundantly.

Of all the things I've said, done, and experienced in my life, God has allowed me to no longer be afraid or ashamed to talk about them. He has not only forgiven me, but freed me from the bondage of secrets, lies, and the games of life I learned to play. Painful as it's been, and wounded as I've felt, if my telling it will expose the lies of Satan, my pain was worth it. If my stories can help save one soul from the pits of deceit and hell, my pain was worth it. If my being talked about will stop one woman from being abused, my pain was worth it. If my telling my story stops one woman from continuing the cycle of abuse, then my pain was worth it. If telling my story stops abuse for another generation, all my pain and suffering was worth it.

This book is to all women and for all women. Know this. It's time for the cycles of secrets, covering up for others, and remaining in bondage of the past to stop. It's time to stop watching women sacrifice themselves, being wounded only for someone to say to them, "I could have told you this would happen." Then why didn't you tell it? Why would you want another person, be it friend or foe, to experience the pain and humiliation you've experienced. Why wouldn't you help others avoid being hurt if you could? Why won't you tell it? Wouldn't you want someone to tell you? Wouldn't you want someone to tell your child how to avoid pain? So why won't you help someone else's child by telling it? Well, "If you can't tell it, Let Me Tell it."

CHAPTER 1

A Thirst That Only God Can Quench

(In the Book of St. John, Chapter 4)** After Jesus left Judaea, he went again to Galilee because he said he must go through Samaria. Upon his arrival to Samaria, being tired he went to Jacob's well to sit. While sitting, a woman of Samaria came to the well to draw water. Jesus asked her to give him a drink. She obviously wasn't used to Jewish men talking with her (at least in public), so she questioned him about asking her for a drink since he was a Jew. Jesus answered and told her if she knew the gift of God and who asked her for a drink, she would have asked him for a drink and he would have given her living water.

Since this woman did not know Jesus, she didn't understand he was offering her an opportunity to repent, and receive the Holy Spirit. When he spoke of the gift of God, in (Acts 2:38) Peter replied, "Repent and be baptized, every one of you, in the name of Jesus Christ for the forgiveness of your sins. And you will receive the gift of the Holy Spirit."

It was clear she didn't understand what he was talking about because she told him that she had nothing to draw water with. Jesus, knowing all about the woman, he told her to go get her husband. She told him she didn't have one. Jesus then acknowledges to her, that not only is she honest in saying she didn't have a husband, she has had five husbands and the one she was currently with was not her husband.

The interesting thing is that Jesus met her at the well not because he was thirsty. He knew she would be at the well. I've often wondered if she met men at the well or on her way to and from the well. Regardless, what she was thirsting for was not water. She was empty and needed to feel whole and complete. Like most women, she thought she could fill that void and be complete if she had a man.

The end of the story tells about how this woman went out telling everyone about the man she had met at the well. Today, we call that

Evangelism. And to think, some people say women aren't suppose to preach.

"If You Can't Tell It, Let Me Tell It!"

This story hit home with me. I too have had two husbands and I don't believe either one of them were mine. As I thought about this woman I thought about myself. There was a time in my life when I was "thirsty." I was like this woman and I was not thirsty for water. I, like this woman thought my thirst could be quenched by a man. I, like this woman was mistaken.

There was a void I was trying to fill. I thought a man could fill it for me. I thought I was thirsty for honesty, truth, stability, affection, and happiness with another human being. I was thirsting, empty and needed an intimate relationship that would have trust, integrity, safety, comfort, and consistency. There were many things I wanted and needed, but it wasn't with a man. I just thought it was. The relationship I longed for was a love that only God could give. This is the kind of love that no man can give except he has the love of Christ in his heart. He has to live a life that reflects his love for God in word and in deed.

I was giving myself for what I thought was love. Later to find that I was only being used to satisfy the physical need of that person for a period of time. After thirsting so long, it became clear the void could only be filled by God. Love is more than a four letter word that is spoken. Love is an action and can be felt when sincerely given. It took years for me to comprehend what I knew, but had not put into words, or written it on paper. No one will ever love you like God does.

Somebody once told me my love was dangerous. At times I thought loving someone was too painful because of getting hurt all the time. It was because when I loved, there were no boundaries to my love. When I loved someone, I expressed it, showed it, and I would do whatever I could so the person would not doubt it. But my love dangerous, I didn't think so. I didn't understand what he meant until now.

Nowadays, I understand sincere love can be dangerous to someone who has never received it nor been able to sincerely give it. This kind of love is not easily handled by someone who does not identify with the power of love, because God is love. Therefore it can cause one to fear, become insecure, and feel there is an ulterior motive as to your level of love shown towards them. Therefore, there will always be a lack of trust. Where there is no trust the relationship will not survive.

I understand that love shared to the fullest measure with the wrong person can be dangerous for the person giving it, and especially hazardous to the person who is receiving it. It can be overwhelming and too much to handle. This is what overwhelms me about the love Christ has for everyone. Because of his love, I can't stop loving because my love has been abused and taken for granted in the past.

In the course of my thirsting for the love of Christ and the fullness of the Holy Spirit, I went through the motions for years. All I really needed was to return to my first love. My first love knew me before I was formed in my mother's womb. My first love is my heavenly father who also chose me before the foundation of the world according to his word.

God, my heavenly father who loves me so much, that he protected me while I was in my sin. His protection was all around me when my life was in danger. His love was around me when I thought I would lose my mind. God who loves me so much he sacrificed his only son to show his love for me. He loves me so much that now I can truly love myself. I no longer thirst for the love of man. I have the love of God and his love is more than enough.

I don't claim to know everything, and I never will. What I do know is this. I was trying to fill a void that was only temporarily satisfied. You might wonder how I knew it was only temporary. I know because I had to keep going back trying to fill it over and over again. Oh, maybe it was with a different person, but I was taking the same test. It may have been a different drink, but I was taking the same test. It may have been a different brand of cigarette I smoked, but believe me, it was the same test. Not only was I taking the same test, I kept failing it too. The only way the void was filled and the thirst was quenched was when I stopped running from Jesus. I ran to Jesus instead. Believe me, Jesus is the only one who can fill the void permanently and completely.

Nobody every explained this longing and feeling of a void I had. I never even heard about it until I heard it taught in Dallas, Texas. Then I begin to study about it in the book of Ephesians. In the book of Ephesians 1:1-5, the word of the Lord says, "Paul, an apostle of Jesus Christ by the will of God, to the saints which are at Ephesus, and to the faithful in Christ Jesus: Grace be to you, and peace, from God our Father, and from the Lord Jesus Christ. Blessed be the God and Father of our Lord Jesus Christ, who hath blessed us with all spiritual blessings in heavenly places in Christ:

According as he hath chosen us in him before the foundation of the world, that we should be holy and without blame before him in love: Having predestinated us unto the adoption of children by Jesus Christ to himself, according to the good pleasure of his will, To the praise of the glory of his grace, wherein he hath made us accepted in the beloved."

Our spirits were with God before we had a body of flesh. When we were born, we were born into the natural world of sin. As time goes on, we have a longing, or a void. We oftentimes express it by saying something is missing within us. The missing element is that personal relationship and fellowship with God. As a result, I needed restoration. I needed to return to my first love. Once we accept Jesus Christ as our personal Savior, that relationship is re-established and the thirsty void is filled through and by the power of the Holy Spirit.

There is nothing more powerful than repenting and returning to your first love. The most awesome thing is that Jesus is waiting to show you that he loves you. My prayer for you is that you become like the people the Samaritan woman left the well and witnessed to. You will not believe that God loves you because I told you, but I pray you will come to know the full extent of which he loves you. I pray you personally experience his love. My prayer is that you allow Jesus to quench your thirst so that you may never thirst again. My prayer is that when he does, you too can say "Let Me Tell It."

CHAPTER 2

Repent

(**I**n the Book of St. John, Chapter 8**)** Early one morning when Jesus was at the Mount of Olives, he went to the temple to sit and teach the people. While he was there, the scribes and Pharisees brought a woman to him who was caught in the act of committing adultery. They justified this by quoting the law of Moses which commanded that she be stoned, but asked if he would save her to tempt him in order to accuse him. Jesus stooped down, wrote on the ground with his finger, and acted as though he didn't hear them. When they continued to ask him, he stood up and said, "He that is without sin among you, let him first cast a stone at her."

And again, he stooped down, wrote something else on the ground, and people's conscience convicting them left one at a time. Jesus stood up again; he saw that no one was there except the woman. So he asked her where those who had accused her were. When she said there were none who accused her, he told her neither did he. He told her to go and sin no more.

"If You Can't Tell It, Let Me Tell It!"

This story has been told over the years, and there is one question that always comes up. Since this woman was said by her accusers to have been caught in the very act of adultery, where was the man? The last time I heard about adultery, two people were involved in order to have committed it. Even then, all the blame went towards the woman.

Although society makes it sound as though adultery is the worse sin one can commit, I've not read in the word of God that sins rank from 1 – 10 with number one being the worse or number ten being the least. The truth of the matter is that God holds me accountable for every sin. Sin is sin. Right is right and wrong is wrong. I heard someone say, "It's like being a little pregnant. You're either pregnant or you're not."

Earlier I made reference to having a ceremony that I thought was a marriage. I called it that because the ceremony was beautiful. It was the relationship that was so ugly. After months of emotionally growing further and further apart, the existing became a way of life. We were smiling and pretending in public while riding to and from places without speaking two words to each other. As a child, we called it the "Silent Treatment." It was draining the life out of both of us. I've never been good at pretending, so it didn't work very well with me. I wasn't happy and I didn't care who knew it in public, at church or in private. The problem was I didn't tell anyone about what was taking place behind closed doors. I tried to deal with it the only way I knew how. And it wasn't the right way.

I had an "I'll get you back" mentality. So, when I heard the person I had a ceremony with was cheating, I waited to see if it was true. After receiving phone calls from women, after the physical and verbal fights, and finally, after having proof that there was adultery going on, I made a choice. It was the wrong choice. I decided to cheat too. I do not use his cheating as an excuse for my wrong doing. I was just as wrong as he was. It was sin just the same. Not to mention the woman always ends up with the worse reputation between the two.

When that relationship ended, I admit I didn't allow God to fix it. Nor did I allow him to fix me in the process. I made a choice to do what I wanted to do. Therefore, I created a mess. By the end of the relationship, I paid for the mess I made. Yet, through it all, God is so good. Eventually the person and I had the opportunity to talk about what transpired between us. We both admitted we didn't handle the situation the way we should have. We repented to each other, repented to God, and were able to move on with our lives. He is now remarried with a family and God is blessing him. For that, I am grateful. I learned many valuable lessons from the experience. I learned even more about myself.

The second time around, as the song said, "I was going to make it better than the first time." I was not going to make the same mistakes and fall into the trap of doing what was being done to me. This time I was going to make sure if this relationship didn't work, it wouldn't be on me. Not realizing that making it appear as though I would or was committing adultery was just as bad as committing it to the person who believed it. Perceptions are real to the person who perceives them. I embarked on another course of destruction. Only this time, I was the one being accused of committing adultery. Let me tell you about my accusers and the God who delivered me from ever wanting to sin again.

Flirting is what I was accused of, and I could be flirtatious at times. When I did flirt, I was very conscience of it. Being raised to be nice to everyone, and since I smile a lot, I've been accused of being flirtatious all of my life. Since my job was as an advertising Sales Representative for a yellow page company, I began to use my personality to make sales. I was nice to people, and I let them think what they wanted. That was wrong.

My attitude was bad and since I was accused of flirting, I decided to do just that. I knew I wasn't going to back up anything discussed that didn't concern the signed contract. I wasn't going to do what anyone told me to do. I had an "It's all about me" attitude. Then I went into survival mode. That attitude was just what the devil was waiting on.

I worked for an advertising company selling ads. I had a diverse group of customers which included men and women. No matter how I invited or asked for support by going out on customer calls with me, it never happened. Still, I was constantly accused of being with men in some way. I was working with a lot of male customers like contractors, attorneys, small retail store owners. Although I was accused of it, I didn't sleep with any of them. And as long as I knew, they knew, and God knew, I didn't care what anyone else thought about me. Not to mention, no matter what I did to prove I wasn't cheating, the accusations continued. So, I got tired of trying to prove otherwise.

One night, I went to meet a potential customer, Pat, a photographer. Before leaving, the meeting, I noticed my wallet was missing. Rich, another potential customer who was a contractor, gave me his jacket since I had not worn my coat that day. Pat offered to help me backtrack to the places I visited earlier. That day, I visited over seven locations. During the search I lost track of time, and I didn't have my cell phone. After hours of searching, Pat and I returned to the restaurant to find it closed. Rich was not where to be found.

On the way to the house, I was searching for the wallet between the seats and on the floor of the car. All of a sudden, I saw lights flashing behind me. I was pulled over by a Police Officer. I explained to him that I had lost my wallet and was on my way to the house. He checked my license plate and insurance card to verify I was who I said I was; he let me go with a warning. Of course, when I went in the house I was accused of being drunk and having an affair. I was not detained nor arrested for drunk driving because I wasn't drunk.

When I reached the house, I was afraid to go inside so I sat in the car for a period of time. Once I went in, the cursing, yelling, and screaming started. Rich had called and said the jacket he loaned me had his house keys in it. Yes, I had the jacket, but there were never any keys in the jacket. I believe it was a way for the devil to make it look like something it wasn't.

That night, I was called so many names and cursed out so bad, I can't even remember all the names I was called. There were so many names I was called until eventually the words were just noise to me. They became a blur. I tried to explain, but was constantly screamed and cursed at so I just shut up. The next afternoon, I received a phone call from a restaurant manager letting me know my wallet had been found. To verify my story, I decided to take one of the trusted relatives with me to pick up the wallet as a witness to my story the night before. Even that didn't matter. I was still humiliated and embarrassed for having to take someone with me as if I was a child.

Despite the abuse, despite seeking couples counseling on more than one occasion, despite quitting the sales job, it wasn't good enough. Despite getting a new job paying $15,000 less a year to be in an office setting, it wasn't good enough. Making many sacrifices, including living underground in a basement, it wasn't good enough. Despite being faithful to someone who hung out every night himself at a beer establishment, none of it was good enough. Instead, I was belittled about the job I took at a recycling company. The relationship situation continued to deteriorate. It didn't look good, feel good, or sound good. But it was good for me.

See, the first time I was married (the ceremony) I didn't give God a chance to change or fix the situation at all. I thought I could cheat bigger and better not realizing it put me in a worse situation. This time, I can honestly say that there is not a man in this state who can say if I am a male or female. The opinion of others might differ because of my behavior which I have never denied was inappropriate. This time my actions made it appear as though I would cheat even though I wasn't. I am thankful to God I didn't. I'm even more thankful that God wouldn't allow me to.

This person acting out wasn't me. I've been taught that everyone does not bring out the best in you. I knew this wasn't really who I was and couldn't continue to exist like that. I wanted to live and feel alive again. Although I tried to change and make things better between us, it didn't get better. I wasn't trying to make it better because I loved the man any more. It was because my understanding was different. I understood that I did not make a vow to the man. I made a VOW to God about the man. My commitment was to God to keep my vow. If anyone was going to break it, it wasn't going to be me.

As difficult as it was, I had humbled myself. I repented to him and to God for everything I could think of. I returned to my first love, which was God. When I repented, I was determined that nothing and/or nobody would ever separate me from the love of God ever again. Not even myself. The changes made in my life were not me but by the power of the Holy Spirit working on me and through me. God changed me and I knew it within myself.

One morning as I was leaving for work, I was told about the divorce papers. He said he was confused about me now. When I asked why, he said because I had changed and I was different. I told him I had accepted my call into the Ministry over eight months ago. I explained to him that what had been going on between us had nothing to do with him. I had been running from God and had decided to run to him instead. I looked at him and told him, 'Whatever was going on with you has nothing to do with me." He had to figure that out for himself. After looking at him, I smiled and said, "Do what you have to do. I'm going to work." I kissed him, as I always did, and went to work.

I found that once a man has in his heart and mind that he's not going to trust or forgive you, it doesn't matter what you do. He will not trust you and it won't matter to him. It didn't matter that we had separate phone lines and separate bank accounts and I didn't fuss about it. I didn't think it was right, but I wasn't going to argue about it. It didn't matter that I lost my wallet and took a witness when it was found to verify why I was out so late. It didn't matter that 911 calls for domestic violence were on record. It didn't matter that I was out late many nights because I didn't want to go to that house to be cursed out and/or ignored until it was time to have sex.

It didn't matter that I repented for everything I could think of. It didn't matter that the night I was served with divorce papers I was with two other women and we were praying for our husbands. It didn't matter that I anointed everything he touched in and around the house for the Holy Spirit to cover and protect us. It didn't matter that I had planted faith seeds in church for his deliverance of alcoholism and abusive ways. It didn't matter that I paid tithes for him because I didn't want God to cut him off from his blessings. In the end, I didn't care if it mattered to him. I wasn't doing it for him. I was doing it to honor the vow I made to God.

It may never matter to anyone else, but I'm glad and thankful it mattered to God.

The change taking place was refreshing. Jesus had not only forgiven me, the Holy Spirit had comforted me and taught me to be true to myself and God. I was delivered from drinking, smoking, cursing, and hanging out. God didn't allow any harm to come to me while I was hanging out and I don't take it lightly. I knew nothing about where I had relocated and anything could have happened to me. Yet, God loved me so much that he protected me even from myself. It wasn't that I had not been taught right from wrong. The choices made, bad as they might have been, were mine.

Only by the mercy and grace of God was I afforded the opportunity to repent. I thank him for the space to repent and the mind to recognize I needed to. To God I give all the Glory! If you are reading this book and have not taken the time to repent, now would be as good a time as any. Repent and give your life to Christ. If you are ready, right now you can repent and be forgiven of your sins. People can tell you many ways they think you should do it but I am going to tell you what the word of God says.

Accepting Christ as you personal Savior is this simple. In Romans 10:9-10, the word of God says, "That if thou shalt confess with thy mouth the Lord Jesus, and shalt believe in thine heart that God hath raised him from the dead, thou shalt be saved. For with the heart man believeth unto righteousness; and with the mouth confession is made unto salvation." If you have opened your mouth, confessed, and repeated these scriptures and truly believe in your heart what your mouth just spoke, you are saved according to the word of God in Jesus' name.

Don't let anyone tell you or convince you otherwise. Pray and ask the Lord to lead you to a church home where you can be taught more about him. Ask him to fill you by baptizing you in the Holy Spirit with the evidence of speaking in tongues as spoken of in the book of Acts, Chapter 2. God loves you and in the book of Romans, Chapter 8:1-2 the word of God says, "There is therefore now no condemnation to them which are in Christ Jesus, who walk not after the flesh, but after the Spirit. For the law of the Spirit of life in Christ Jesus hath made me free from the law of sin and death."

Woman of God, be free. For when Jesus forgives you and makes you free, you are no longer held in the bondage of your past. God is true to his word and you are unquestionably forgiven. Woman of God, go forth from this moment on knowing and walking in the liberation of Christ. May you find comfort in knowing that God is your father, Jesus Christ is your personal Savior, and the Holy Spirit is your comforter and teacher. God loves you and I love you. Woman of God, Be Blessed in the Name of Jesus!

CHAPTER 3

What A Woman Of God Will Do

(**I**n the Book of 1 Samuel, Chapter 25) There is a man by the name of Nabal, whose possessions were in Carmel, sheep, and goats. Nabal's wife was Abigail. The bible describes her as a woman of good understanding, and was of a beautiful countenance. However, Nabal was described as churlish and evil in his actions, deeds, and activities.

When David heard that Nabal sheared his sheep, he sent out ten young men to greet Nabal in his name and bless him by saying, "And thus shall ye say to him that liveth in prosperity, peace be both to thee, and peace be to thine house, and peace be unto all that thou hast."

David knew that while Nabal's shepherds were with them, they didn't hurt them, and nothing they had in their possession was missing while they were with them. The servants of David asked that Nabal find favor for him and his shepherds. David was coming in about a day, so David's prayer was for Nabal to be kind to him and his servants. When David's servants spoke to Nabal, he asked the servants, "Who is David?" Nabal then accused David of possibly being a servant who could have escaped from his master.

David's men returned and told him what Nabal had said, and David was prepared to do battle and kill Nabal, but one of the young men told Abigail, Nabal's wife, how the servants came to salute Nabal and his behavior in turn was inappropriate and unacceptable. The servant explained that David's men were good to them and didn't take anything from them, and protected them night and day while they were together keeping the sheep. The servant knew that David was going to consider killing Nabal and that Nabal wouldn't listen to reason. So, Abigail rushed to take food and many supplies to David and his servants. She sent one of her servants before her and didn't tell her husband Nabal. While coming down trying not to be seen, David and his men came down towards her, and she met them.

David spoke to Abigail about Nabal not being appreciative of his kindness towards his sheppards. David let her know that he was going to destroy everything Nabal had by the morning. When Abigail saw David, she fell before David on her face, bowed herself to the ground, fell at his feet, and said, "Upon me, my lord, upon me let this iniquity be" meaning let the wickedness, evil, sin, and injustice that Nabal did be placed upon her instead of him. She spoke to David about Nabal and what his name meant. His name meant fool and how folly is with him. He was thoughtless, reckless, and displayed thoughtless or reckless behavior, an undertaking that is excessively costly or extravagant, especially one that leads to financial loss or ruin.

Abigail begins to pray for David not only to spare Nabal's life but for David to stay the man of God he was and take the blessings that she brought to share with his servants that followed him. Abigail spoke to David about him being pursued and the enemies wanting to kill him, but that David was protected because the Lord fought his battles. She asked that when the Lord had done his part that David not forget her.

Then David blessed the Lord for sending Abigail to meet him, received her advice, he then blessed her for helping him to remember that God will fight his battles. David knew that the Lord had kept him from hurting her and killing Nabal. He received her gift of goods, sent her away in peace to her house because he had received and accepted what she had said.

Upon Abigail's return home, she found Nabal having a feast in the house and he was drunk. She didn't tell him anything until the next morning. When Nabal was sober and Abigail told him what had happened, he became very bitter, angry, and hardhearted. The bible says "his heart died within him, and he became as a stone." About ten days later, the Lord smote Nabal, and he died. Eventually, Abigail became David's wife.

"If You Can't Tell It, Let Me Tell It!"

One of the hardest times in my life was realizing that I had entered into a contractual agreement with an alcoholic. I thought I was in a relationship with someone who said he had accepted Christ as his personal Savior. Three days after relocating, I realized that although a person confesses their salvation, it doesn't mean they've been fully delivered.

Being married to an alcoholic is a scary life. You never know what mood they'll be in when they come home or while they're at home. Regardless, the realization of being in a relationship with someone who is now showing that they are not who you thought they were, is frightening. My first frightening experience turned out to be a violent one. It happened three days after I arrived.

I was downstairs working on my resume' while this person, unbeknownst to me, was upstairs drinking. While I was working on my resume, he entered the room and started talking to me. The sad part is, I don't remember how the conversation started but it turned into an argument. As the argument continued, it became worse.

During the course of the argument, my computer was knocked off my lap and I was called the "B" word. This "B" word didn't stand for Beauty either. I stood up and asked, "What did you call me?" I asked not because I didn't hear what was said, but I was shocked at what was said. This person obviously was showing me what I had to look forward to in the relationship. Not only was the word repeated, I was slapped in the face as well.

The next thing I knew, a physical fight was taking place. When I tried to run, I was grabbed, held down, and punched in my face and my mouth. Finally, I was able to run out of the house and across the street to a parked police car. When I looked up, I was being chased. After we talked to the Police officer, I was accused of starting the fight. To my surprise, the police officer told me that since the 911 terror attacks, the number of domestic violent calls had increased because people were more stressed out than before.

When I explained that I had only been in town three days and that I had nowhere to go, the officer asked where I was from. I told him I was from Texas and not only did I not have any family here, my car had not arrived. I had no way of going any place. The officer was nice, but I was seeking some answers about what to do.

To my surprise, the officer admitted that he and his wife had been arguing much more lately since the terrorist attacks. I was even more surprised when he recommended that I consider a cooling off period for the person instead of having him arrested. This made me feel like I had no other options, so that is what I did. I had no idea it wouldn't be the last time the police would be called.

The next morning, it took me over two hours of talking before there was any admission of being wrong for the violence and abuse. At first I was told that it was a reaction to my actions. One trait of an abuser is they will not take responsibility. They blame you for their abusive and inappropriate behavior.

During the conversation I was told that I would now have to take care of myself. So, during the entire time of the relationship, one car payment was made on my behalf. After I found a job, there was no contribution to help me pay any personal bills whatsoever. I was given a year's membership at a gym but was not allowed to choose the gym of my choice. Although appreciative for having a place to stay, it was always clearly communicated that it wasn't my house. Everyone who lived there let me know it.

I had been informed that I was now responsible for taking care of myself and I needed to hurry and find a job. I remember feeling so afraid, very nervous, all alone, and too embarrassed to tell anyone. Before relocating I was not working and there was no income being provided. I sold everything, cashed in my 401K, and had spent all my savings. Not a smart thing to do, I admit, but a lesson well worth learning.

There is a story in the book of Luke, Chapter 18 that talks about a rich man wanting to follow Jesus. In trying to find out what he needed to do in order to follow Jesus, he spoke of knowing the commandments but only mentioned a few. They were: Do not commit adultery, Do not kill, Do not steal, Do not bear false witness, and Honor thy father and thy mother. He then said that he had kept them all since he was a youth. In Luke 18:21-22, the word of God says, "Now when Jesus heard these things, he said unto him, Yet lackest thou one thing: sell all that thou hast, and distribute unto the poor, and thou shalt have treasure in heaven: and come, follow me." My lesson was an expensive lesson, but a lesson all the same. See, Jesus never said sell all you have and follow a man. He said "Follow Me."

Since, my car had not arrived, and I didn't know my way around to look for a job, one of the relatives took me to interviews. Two weeks after being in town, my car finally arrived. However, my safety was still in the back of my mind. It later became more evident and later resulted in emotional and physical distress.

Later that month, I noticed night after night that he would come in and pass out on the couch. I sought the advice of a relative who told me he was not an alcoholic. He just drinks with his friends. The truth was that it was more than a social drink. He would go out and drink with his friends everyday, come home, drink more and many times he would pass out. He was an alcoholic, and I was with him.

Soon, I noticed a pattern of my being left alone for hours at a time. What made it worse was I was in a basement. I felt as if I couldn't breathe at times. It was dark with one small window in the bedroom. When I commented to some of the family members about being left alone everyday in the basement, I was told people have a right to hang out with their friends. I agreed. There was just an issue of being married now. I felt if any hanging out for hours should have been taking place, it should have been with me.

To my disappointment, about a month later, I found the hangout. It was a hole in the wall liquor store where several men hung out. There was no bar or sitting area found. They were in the storage room sitting on crates and carts. I thought to myself, they might as well be under a tree with a couch and a card table. The room was dark and the store owners didn't seem to have a problem with it. I couldn't believe it. I was thinking, "My God, this is what was being preferred over spending time with me? Oh My God! What is this? What have I gotten myself into and who is this person I am with?"

This was the beginning of my being sent into a downward spiral of disappointment and depression. I was looking for a job day after day, being left alone night after night, but expected to have sex no matter what I thought or about how I felt. I felt more like a roommate. I sure never felt like I was a wife. The only difference between me being someone's play toy was a legal piece of paper. I was hurt, disappointed, and angry. No matter how I tried to talk about it, I was told what I wanted to hear and soon the behavior started all over again. It was a vicious cycle that looked as though there was no end in sight.

Instead of going back home, reaching out for the help of my family and friends, I was determined that I was not going to just sit by and be treated like I didn't exist. When my car arrived, I purposed to prove that point to everyone. I wasn't going to tolerate the abusive treatment and sit back and do nothing. I felt that since I had always taken care of myself, it wouldn't be a problem. My problem was I did not know anyone or my way around. But, since I learned fast, I was going for it.

In my mind, I figured as soon as I have my car and a better job, I'd have him looking for me. I wanted to let him know how it felt. With all the anger and bitterness building, I rebelled. I didn't just rebel against what he said, I rebelled against God. The resentment and anger continued to build. I wasn't going to listen to what anyone wanted me to do. I backslid and went back to what I knew, but didn't help the situation at all.

After finding a job in sales, I met new people every day. The company would have parties and before I knew it, I was smoking and drinking again. It was my way of escaping and not dealing with what was happening to me in the relationship. I would hang out until all hours of the night sometimes.

I didn't care what anyone thought or had to say about it. It's interesting how the opinions about hanging out changes when the person hanging out is a woman. All of a sudden, it wasn't such a good idea to hang out with friends anymore.

Most nights, I came home to be cursed and I didn't care because I thought, "What do you care? I'm taking care of myself like just like you told me to." I didn't want to have sex anymore, so I would drink to be able to deal with being touched by someone who wasn't showing me any attention or spending any time with me otherwise. One night, I returned to the house and my mother had called. That didn't help. It made me even angrier than I was before.

I said, "What in the world do you think my mother is going to do, whip me?" This didn't help my level of respect for this person. I thought to myself, "What a wimp you are to call and tell my mother on me." I did calm down enough to speak with my mother, who of course was afraid because I was hanging out so late. She asked me to be careful because it was dangerous to be out so late alone. She was right, but as soon as I hung up the phone, I looked at the person and laughed in his face. I was out of control. I knew it, and for a while, I didn't care. I had a hard time conceiving that I had given up everything to live like this. I was not dealing well with the way I was treated. Yes, it was my decision and I wasn't forced into it, but now that I was in it, I didn't want to be.

I am thankful to God that no matter how out of control we both became, no matter how we acted out with each other, something inside of me wouldn't allow me to continue the destructive behavior. See, I had been saved and knew that God had a calling on my life. I just didn't want to accept it. I ran from it for years somehow thinking I was too bad of a person for God to use me. I knew years ago that I was supposed to preach the word of God, but I didn't want to. I thought it was about me. Now I know that once I gave my life to God, it was no longer my own.

It seemed as though the hours of darkness was overtaking me. I was in bed crying, looking up at the low, mildewed ceiling in a small room. The room had dark brown walls that looked as though they were closing in on me. I cried out and began to talk out loud to the Lord. I didn't care anymore about who heard me or what they thought. I said, "Lord, help me! Help me! I can't keep living like this. I feel like I'm dying. If have to keep living like this, I'd rather be dead." I am not sure how long I cried that night, but within a few minutes a small voice said, "I've been waiting on you to die."

I didn't understand it at the time, but the next day when I woke up I didn't feel the same. I went to work and made several sales calls. One stop was DeMatteo Salvage Company. DeMatteo's is a family owned company that has been in business for over 80 years. The company is run by owner's Joseph and Carmine DeMatteo. Their sister, Amalia DonVito DeMatteo, is the Office Manager. After meeting Joseph, he sent me to speak with Amalia.

When I first met her, she told me she didn't have time to speak with me. I remember standing and looking at her with a smile on my face. Then she looked at me and said, "You have a very pretty smile. Go ahead and tell me your pitch." By the end of my conversation with her she told me about her being too busy to really take time with me. See, they had recently lost a brother in a car accident and her office assistant had resigned.

As I looked around, I said, "You should hire me." We both laughed. I explained how I was looking for another job and could bring her my resume' and give her references the next day. I saw God begin to move on my behalf within a few minutes. By the next week, I was working there. What I thought was a potential sale, turned out to be a place where God settled me in order to get me focused on him.

The DeMatteo's are an incredible family and were the nicest people I had met since my move. They worked hard and helped anyone in any way they could. I worked with them for over a year. During that time, this family treated me as if I were their family. They made sure I had everything I needed and even fed me everyday. I was never asked pay a dime for a meal or anything else I needed. Joey and Carmine were like fathers to me and Amalia was like a mother. God placed me there and he started to heal me there. This family became my family away from home. I'm still grateful to them.

I kept thinking about that voice saying "I've been waiting on you to die." As I began to get focused on God, I began to study his word again. I prayed and recommitted my life to God. While studying one night, I remembered in 2 Corinthians 5:16-18 the word of God says, "Wherefore henceforth know we no man after the flesh: yea, though we have known Christ after the flesh, yet now henceforth know we him no more. Therefore if any man be in Christ, he is a new creature: old things are passed away; behold, all things are become new. And all things are of God, who hath reconciled us to himself by Jesus Christ, and hath given to us the ministry of reconciliation."

Devetta Arnold

God didn't change the situation or the relationship for the better while I was there. God did change me. I learned what a woman will do when she loves God, makes a commitment to him, and keeps it. I sometimes articulate it as having a "Nevertheless" moment like Jesus did in the garden of Gethsemane. (Matthew 26:39), the word of God says, "And he went a little farther, and fell on his face, and prayed, saying, O my Father, if it be possible, let this cup pass from me: nevertheless not as I will, but as thou wilt."

I could have called my parents and friends to come get me and take me home, but I didn't. Say what you will and think what you must. I've learned a lot about what a woman will do. Most of all I learned what I could do and endure with the help of the Lord. As I continue to grow in him each day, I am learning more about what my God can and will do when we reach out to him.

CHAPTER 4

If You Can Just Get To Him

(In the book of Mark, Chapter 5)** There was a certain woman who had been bleeding for twelve years. After many visits to the doctors, she spent all her money and was said to have gotten worse instead of better. When she heard of Jesus, she began to press/push her way toward him from behind to touch his garment. She heard of his healing power, so she said if she could just touch his clothes, she would be whole. Immediately the blood was dried up; and she felt in her body that she was healed.

Jesus knowing immediately that virtue had gone out of him, turned around and asked his disciples who had touched his clothes? The disciples knew there were many people trying to get to him, but the woman became fearful and fell down in front of him. She told him it was her who had touched him. He called her "Daughter" and told her that her faith had made her whole. In the beginning of the story she was the woman with the issue. By the end of her time with Jesus she was "Daughter."

"If You Can't Tell It, Let Me Tell It!"

One day, I couldn't stop crying and my mother was called to calm me down. I had become hysterical because I knew that in spite of all that was going on around me, my soul was longing for Jesus to touch me. For the first time in my life, I didn't feel his presence around me. I felt like my soul was dying within me. I needed to be back in fellowship with him but I didn't know how. After being looked at like I was crazy all the time and getting cursed out almost on a daily basis, I lost it and began to cry out to the Lord.

The truth of the matter is that I too had an issue. As a matter of fact, I had a lot of issues. My nickname was always "Mama" to my mom and dad and for years it was my special name. However, as I went through the different experiences "Mama" grew up. I feel like she died in that basement and she no longer existed. This was a good thing. I was independent, but I was also very spoiled. If wanted things to happen, when they didn't, I did what I could to make them happen. If I didn't like what was happening, I could run away from it or get out of it. It was time to face reality about what I was running from. Not only was I running from dealing with myself, I was running from God and what he had called me to do.

Since there didn't seem to be a way to calm me down, my mother in Los Angeles was called. She was too far away to come get me, so all she could do was talk to me. She and one of her friends tried to calm me down. I could hear them, but I couldn't stop crying. Finally I remember my mother saying, "Devetta, if you could just stop and pray I know you'll be alright." She told me to calm down again. She must have been praying for me because there was a peace that came over me. Finally, I was able to calm down. My mother's words were some of the most powerful words that she has ever spoken to me. I love her for it and will never forget that moment. Those words not only lifted my spirit, and my self esteem, they empowered me. I focused on God and began to pray.

God had placed me in a situation where I couldn't run any more. Nor did I want to run anymore. The real issue was I needed to grow up. I needed to accept what God had told me to do years ago. So, after I had calmed down, that night I decided to re-commit my life to Christ. I had not found a church home, but I was pressing my way Sunday after Sunday seeking and searching. Each Sunday I would visit another church. All that mattered was my determination to get where God wanted me.

It wasn't long after that when my desire to do the will of God became stronger. I said, "Lord, I'm not running from what you want me to do anymore. I love you and no matter what you decide to do with my life, it's yours now." This time I knew there was no turning back and I didn't want to. God began to change me to the point where I knew I was no longer the same person. I was different than I had ever been. One day, Amalia looked at me and said, "This is amazing. I have literally sat here and watched you change right before my very eyes." I had become new because God had reconciled me back to him by the blood of Jesus according to his word.

There was no more acting out or rebelling again God because of the way people were treating me. I totally surrendered my life to Christ fully and completely. I began looking for a church home, humbled myself before the Lord to the point of one day becoming just like Abigail. I found myself asking God to put the person's sin who was abusing me on me so his soul wouldn't be lost. I was fasting, praying and studying the word of

God on a daily basis. I stayed focused and I was determined to live for God.

Every night I would bow down before the Lord and pray while sometimes being cursed out at the same time. Still, I kissed him everyday when I would come from work, and again at night before going to bed. This was to keep myself humble. It didn't seem to make sense, nor did it feel good. But it wasn't about me anymore. No matter how I was treated, souls were at risk. Mine was one of them. I determined in my heart and mind that I wouldn't lose my soul for anything or anyone. During that time, being alone in the basement day after day became less and less of a concern for me.

At one point, I was determined to make the relationship work, and I felt like it was killing me. My spirit felt like it was dying and my heart was broken. I kept saying, God, I know you're going to bless me. It seemed like the more I said it, the more broken I became, the worse the situation became. I had been threatened with divorce papers for so long I had become a nervous wreck. I would rush home from church, work, or even the store looking at the time. I was always thinking, "I am going to get cursed out or given divorce papers." That's when I discovered mental/ emotional abuse can be worse than the physical abuse at times.

No one could have told me that I would ever be in a domestic violence relationship. The truth of the matter is this. I was in serious denial. Finally, I had to be honest with myself. I was always blamed for his temper. I was moved and isolated from my entire family. I was cursed out and called names like "Country bumpkin." I was never asked to invite my friends and/or family to come for visits. I was forced to have sex when I was uncomfortable. I was hit, slapped, punched, and choked. I was threatened and accused of cheating. Does any of this sound familiar to you? If it does, you too are in a domestic violence relationship. You should seek help immediately. If it doesn't sound familiar, you are blessed.

I've been told that some people might say I was a fool. Some might even say I got what I deserved. I say that is their opinion and they are entitled to have it. I learned a lot from Abigail. I learned a lot about what a woman will do when she shares her heart with someone she loves and trust enough to share her life with.

Typically, for a woman, there is no limit to her love when she does love. A woman will sacrifice herself not just once but several times. A woman will endure hurt over and over, yet have the capacity to love again. A woman will put herself in harms way to ensure that others she loves aren't harmed. A woman will do for others what she will not do for herself. A woman, who has loved, will love, and continues to love. A woman will love because she was given the will to do so.

It came to the point when all the names I was called didn't matter anymore. I was focused on serving God at any cost. I also knew that God was either going to save him or move me out of the situation all together. I refused to act in an immoral manner or degrade myself again because of the situation I found myself in. As a woman, I thought this experience would break me down, but it ended up being a blessing. As a matter of fact, I am not just a better woman after the experience. I am a Blessed Woman of God and he is not finished working on me yet.

Although none of the relationships gave me what I needed, I didn't give up. My mother was right. I needed to calm down and pray. Finally, a church located at 114 Long Island Avenue in Wyandanch, New York was recommended. The person who told me about the church said, "The Spirit is very high there." I knew that I needed to be where the spirit of the Lord was. The next Sunday I set out to go there for a visit.

The Pastor was preaching and walked towards me and said, "God's got a miracle for you." Pastor Roberts walked around for a few minutes, came back to me and said, "I don't know what your ministry is but you've got one." I thought to myself, "Lord I need a miracle right now. I am not going to run from the ministry any more. I surrender to you. Forgive me and cleanse me from all this unrighteousness and make me whole."

As I sat quietly, Pastor Roberts came back towards me again. This time he said he typically doesn't bother visitors because he doesn't want to make them uncomfortable, but asked if he could pray for me. I stood up and walked towards him as one of the deacons stood with him. As I stood in front of him, he laid his hands on my head and prayed for me. I felt the touch of the Lord through him and after the prayer he prayed, and my life has not been the same.

A couple of months later, I publicly accepted my call into the ministry. My official ordination service was held on "Pentecost Sunday" May 30, 2004 at 6:30 p.m. Today, I am a proud member of the Full Gospel Church of God by Faith, located at 114 Long Island Avenue, Wyandanch, New York, 11798. Pastor Roberts, thank you for allowing God to use you, and thank you for praying for me.

I thank God for blessing me with my mother, Alice Fay Smith. She could have given me many directions to take that night. She chose to direct me back to God. Mommy, thank you for allowing God to use your womb to carry me. Thank you for every pain you took while giving birth and after giving birth to me. Thank you for watching me as I crossed the street to go to church by myself after we moved. Thank you for the yellow ruffled dress with the bells on it I wore that day. Thank you for allowing me to take my first steps back to God; although we both were unaware of that moment being a step towards my destiny.

Thank you for all the sacrifices you made for me. Thank you for doing without so I could have. Thank you for teaching me to do what's right when I didn't want to. Thank you for being a mother I could not only love but respect. Thank you for teaching me to be kind to people even when they aren't kind to me. Thank you for teaching me to always pay my tithes first, no matter what. Thank you for loving me enough to allow me to take this journey without rescuing me. Thank you for standing strong when you knew I was in pain and you couldn't fix it for me.

Thank you for teaching me how to have staying power in spite of what it looks like, sounds like, or feels like. Thank you for being an example of not just a strong black woman, but a woman who allowed God to use your pain to empower my sister Barbara and me. Thank you for telling me that I had to write this book and tell it. This chapter is dedicated to my mother, Alice Faye Smith.

CHAPTER 5

What You Think Will Break You Can

Bless You

(**I**n the Book of II Samuel, Chapter 13)** Absalom was the son of David whose sister's name was Tamar. Tamar was a virgin; and Amnon loved her. Amnon was so irritated, that he fell sick because he knew it would be hard for him to do anything to her. But Amnon had a friend, Jonadab, who was a very clever man. When Jonadab asked Amnon what was wrong with him, he confided in him that he loved Tamar, his brother Absalom's sister. Jonadab came up with a plan for Amnon to ask his father to let his sister Tamar come and prepare a meal and care for him. Amnon laid down, and made himself sick: and when the king came to see him, Amnon asked his request and David sent for Tamar, and told her to go to thy brother Amnon's house, and dress him meat.

Tamar went to her brother Amnon's house; and he was laid down and she prepared a meal for him but he refused to eat. Amnon sent all of the men out of the room and requested that Tamar bring the meat into the chamber so he could eat from her hand. When Tamar did as her brother requested he took hold of her, and told her to come with him. Tamar refused and asked him not to force her because it was wrong, foolish, and she would be disgraced. She told him to ask the King for her and he would honor his request.

Amnon would not listen to her, and since he was stronger than Tamar, he forced her and had sex with him. Afterwards he hated her exceedingly; so much that the hatred became larger than the love he had for her before. And Amnon no longer wanted Tamar in his presence so he told her to get out of his room. She said to him that it was evil to treat her in such a manner, but he didn't care and called one of his servants that ministered unto him, put Tamar out of the room, and bolted the door. When she was grieving, her brother Absalom asked if Amnon had been with her, he told her not to tell anyone. So she didn't tell as he requested. But God knew it, and two years later Amnon was killed by Absalom's servant.

"If You Can't Tell It, Let Me Tell It!"

Several times during the relationship, I felt as though I was being raped or like I was forced to have intercourse when I didn't want to. I remember a time when I was uncomfortable due to my cycle about to start. When I explained, it didn't matter and seemed as though the sex was rougher than usual. Afterwards, I turned my face towards the wall and cried out to God. I told him I couldn't take it anymore. I cried so much, I didn't remember falling asleep that night.

I felt the pain and humiliation Tamar felt and many women all over the world have felt. It doesn't matter if you are married or single; there is still the pain and humiliation. The ironic thing is after Amnon forced her to have sex with him; he had a servant minister to him. Then he had her thrown her out of his room. I always wondered how a person could hurt someone and say they've been forgiven when they haven't asked forgiveness.

The next day while taking a trip to a banquet, I told a friend that God had to move on my behalf. I was tired of being pounced on like an animal. I was tired of having to be exposed to the pornographic movies and sex toys. There were many times I felt sick to my stomach when I was touched. There were times when having sex I would say yes out loud to him and say Lord in my mind in order to keep my sanity. Many times I would go immediately to the restroom to sob and pray. I can only imagine the mental anguish Tamar suffered. I understand now how there are times when the body will function while the mind struggles. I had functioned for over two years.

When I went to the have my annual physical, everything seemed to be going fine until the Physician asked how I was adjusting to married life and relocating from Texas. All of a sudden, tears started flowing until I could hardly speak. The Physician became very concerned. She wanted to prescribe me anti-depressants. She later recommended that I see a therapist. I explained that I had no friends or family in the area. The Physician offered to give me a prescription for the anti-depressants and contact information of a therapist she wanted me to see.

Later that afternoon, I mentioned the concerns of the physician and was cursed out. I was told I didn't need any medication and that I could take some over the counter natural medicine and feel fine. A few hours later, I was handed two bottles of St. John's Wart. I didn't want it and I never took it. My depression was not because I needed medication. I needed to get out of that hole in the ground. I needed to get away from the relationship that was poisoning and killing me. The relationship was toxic. My mind couldn't take it any more and my body was showing the effects of it. I was becoming physically sick.

After being out with one of the Evangelists, she introduced me to one of her friends. We decided to get together that night and pray for our husbands. We finished about midnight. I figured I was either going to be threatened again or cursed out. This time I was wrong. This time, I entered the house and was handed divorce papers. There was no feeling of brokenness. To my surprise, there was a feeling of relief. Instead of crying about the situation, I raised my hand, lifted them in the air, and began to Praise God. I began to thank God. I finally had received them. There was no more worrying or being nervous about getting them.

Earlier, I had been praying about the situation but had no idea God was going to give me an answer that night. At the time, it wasn't the answer I expected or hoped for. However, I trusted that God knew what was best for me. Yes, it was painful, disappointing and not the answer I wanted or thought I would receive, but today, I am thankful to God. It was the answer I needed.

You see, earlier that day, while I was with the Evangelist, I finally broke down crying and shared with her some things I never spoke of before. I cried so hard I could barley talk. When I was able to speak, I told her that God was going to have to do something because I couldn't take any more. I'm thankful that he knows just how much we can handle. This was an experience that I thought would break me mentally, physically, and emotionally. It didn't break me. It turned out to bless me. That is why I know personally that what you think will break you can bless you.

CHAPTER 6

Jesus Was Denied, Yet He Forgave

(In the Book of Genesis, Chapter 29)** Jacob went on a journey east, met some people, and saw a well in the field, where there were three flocks of sheep lying by it. He noticed a stone at the mouth of the well, how the sheep were watered, and returned the stone back at the well's mouth. Jacob asked where they were from, and they said, of Haran. Jacob then asked if they knew Laban the son of Nahor? Since they knew Laban, Jacob asked if he was well. They told him that Laban was well.

While they were speaking, Rachel, Laban's daughter, came with her father's sheep because she kept them. After the cattle were gathered, Jacob would have a chance to speak with Rachel. When he saw her he helped roll the stone from the well's mouth and watered the flock of Laban, who was his mother's brother. Jacob kissed Rachel, and lifted up his voice, and wept. Jacob told Rachel who he was and she ran to tell her father.

Laban heard the news, ran to meet him, embraced and kissed him, and brought him brought him to his house. When Jacob visited Laban, Labon acknowledged they were family. Laban asked Jacob what would he want in wages since he would work for him. Laban had two daughters. The oldest one was Leah and the youngest one was Rachel. Leah was described as tender eyed (not very attractive); but Rachel was described as beautiful and well favored. However, Jacob loved Rachel; and said, I will serve thee seven years for Rachel, thy younger daughter. Laban told Jacob that it would be better for Rachel be given to him than another man.

Although Jacob served seven years for Rachel, it didn't seem long to him because he loved her. The time came when Jacob's seven years were complete. He asked Laban to give him his wife so he could be with her. So Laban gathered everyone together to have a feast. However, that evening Laban brought Leah, the oldest daughter, to Jacob, and her handmaid Zilpah. Jacob slept with Leah and the next morning he saw that it was not Rachel. He asked Laban why he had deceived him by giving him Leah instead of Rachel. Laban told Jacob that in their country the younger daughter is not given in marriage before the older one.

Laban told Jacob that he could have Rachel also if he would serve him another seven years. Once Jacob completed the additional seven years, Laban gave him Rachel his daughter, to wife, and gave Rachel Bilhah, his handmaid, to be her maid. Jacob then went in also unto Rachel; but he loved her more than Leah. He loved her so much he served with Laban another seven years.

When the Lord saw that Leah was hated, he opened her womb so she could become pregnant. Rachel couldn't have children. Leah conceived and had several sons, but Jacob still loved Rachel more.

"If You Can't Tell It, Let Me Tell It!"

This story is a familiar one because most people don't understand how Jacob could not have known that Leah was not Rachel. To me, it is similar to when a man today is married, sleeps with another woman, either gets caught or impregnates the woman other than his wife, then denies having slept with the other woman at all. Even though the parties involved know the truth will come out, they deny it.

I'm not sure if Jacob knew it was Leah or not. I am sure his denying wanting to be with her didn't make her happy. However, Jacob only opposed to being married to her "AFTER" he had slept with her. Not to mention, apparently after marrying Rachel, he continued to sleep with Leah. In my opinion, he wasn't too unhappy. Apparently, Leah must have forgiven him as well.

To deny something or someone and know it is true has an excruciating impact on the person who is being denied. Yet, the person is expected to forgive. This also reminds me of the book of Luke 22:34, the word of God says, "And he said, I tell thee, Peter, the cock shall not crow this day, before that thou shalt thrice deny that thou knowest me," and when Peter did deny Christ, the bible says Jesus turned his face to him and then Peter remembered what he had done. Obviously Peter repented and Jesus forgave him, because in the Book of Acts 8:25, the word of the God says, "When they had testified and proclaimed the word of the Lord, Peter and John returned to Jerusalem, preaching the gospel in many Samaritan villages."

Still, it saddens me that in the year 2004, some women still feel that having children will make a man love them or remain in a relationship with them. It didn't work back in the day and it doesn't work now. Yet today, I still see the games being played while the babies are used to get the men to come around. Yes, I've seen it over and over again. I've even seen it happen in my own family.

It's time for us to be honest with each other and stop continuing the unhealthy cycle of bringing babies in this world with drama taking place in their lives from conception. In Psalm 127:3, the word of the Lord says, "Lo, children are a heritage of the Lord: and the fruit of the womb is his reward." Children are a blessing of the Lord and should be viewed, cared for, and raised as such.

During the younger years in my life, I saw family members and friends in relationships with men where children were conceived. Time after time, I watched and heard some of the men not only deny they had been with the women, they have even denied their children. I heard about it, saw some experience it, but never knew it was preparing me to one day feel the agony, pain and affects of it myself.

One day, I found out I was pregnant. Not only was I not trying to get pregnant, I didn't have a clue I was pregnant. I was eating and sleeping more and thought it was because I was depressed. When I shared this information about the pregnancy I was taken to dinner. What I thought was going to be a celebration turned out to be another disappointment. I will never forget those six words spoken to me in the midst of our conversation. "A baby ain't in my budget." I remember being devastated. I reminded him that I was not someone he had an affair with. I was his wife and this was my first child.

I was then informed about a plan to get out of debt in three years. This was interesting because the plan had not been discussed with me, nor did it include any of my bills. First, I was told the living arrangement in the basement was for a year. That night I was told the year had turned into three years. I thought I would pass out.

When I expressed my unwillingness to raise a child in the condition in which I was currently living, I was offered no other alternative. I was so upset that I left the restaurant, went to the car, and cried. I thought to myself, "this can't be happening to me."

Two days later, due to the emotional stress and strain, I was threatening a miscarriage. To my surprise, I was taken to the doctor and placed on bed rest for two weeks. After two weeks, test results indicated I had lost the baby and would need a DNC. When I made it known that I would have to go in the hospital and have the procedure, I was told a relative would have to take me because of his work schedule. I declined the offer and decided to drive myself. A day before the procedure, I was told that driving myself wouldn't be necessary and time off had been requested.

Some might think the offer was a nice one. I did as well until I realized that I would be left alone the next day because of a jazz concert. Not only would I be left, but an argument occurred because the tickets were purchased months prior to finding out I was pregnant, so I was still expected to attend the concert.

The anger expressed was amazing when I refused to go along. I had just gotten out of the hospital. Again, I was in shock. Maybe I shouldn't have been, but I was. I couldn't believe that in spite of my still bleeding from the procedure that partying was more important than grieving for the loss of my child. However, that is exactly what happened. The other shocking part was that although I wasn't in the house alone, not one person came to ask if I was alright or if I needed anything. Not one person even asked if I needed a glass of water.

The next day a nurse from the hospital had to check on me. I was having an allergic reaction to the anesthesia and felt like I couldn't breathe. She checked on me and followed-up with me the next day. It was so nice of her to check on me because no one else did. I was reminded of the saying, "God always has a ram in the bush."

Just when I thought I couldn't be disrespected any more than I already had, the allegations made when the divorce was filed were beyond belief. After months of hearing in legal documents how awful I was, I decided to tell the entire truth about the domestic violence and cruel and inhumane treatment. After returning from work one day, I opened a letter from the attorney regarding the answer to the papers I filed. I stood in the middle of the floor and read them. I came across the sentence "The Plaintiff does not believe the child was his."

My mind went blank. I can't say how long I stood there. When I came to myself, I was looking up at the ceiling. The first thing I could say was "Jesus." One reason I called on Jesus was because I realized that I didn't remember looking up from the paper. I didn't remember looking up at the ceiling. My mind left. I only remember realizing I was looking up at the ceiling. I didn't remember anything else.

For the first time in my life, I felt like I left reality for a time and came back. I picked up my bible looking desperately for a word from God. In my mind, I could see myself killing him. For two hours I couldn't speak or call anyone. What I felt was beyond hurt, pain, or aching. I couldn't and still can't find a word that explains what I felt. The closest word I could come up with was wounded, but the pain was much worse.

Finally, as I sat, the spirit of the Lord said, "Peter denied Jesus three times." And there was an ease of sorts. I smiled to myself and said, "Thank you Jesus". You may not understand why I found comfort in this, but I'll give you the reason. Every time I would experience something after accepting my call to the ministry, I would find in the bible where it happened to Jesus or something similar happened to him. The word of God is where I found the strength to know that I too could be an over comer. No matter how I was being treated, I could overcome because Jesus did.

After praying a while, I was able to place a phone call to Pastor Ronnie Keener of the St. Matthew's Baptist Church in Foreman, Arkansas. It is the church across the street from my dad's house. It is the church I attended while growing up. People have no idea how powerful the word of God is. Proverbs 18:21 says, "Death and life are in the power of the tongue: and they that love it shall eat the fruit thereof." That scripture came to life right before me. I will never forget the first thing out of Pastor Keener's mouth when I told him what had happened. He said, "Let Him Live." I am so grateful God allowed him to speak a word to me. The word he spoke was a word from God. All I knew was that I was wounded and even the word "wounded" didn't compare to how I felt.

Although I felt the statement was willfully malicious, I thank God for delivering me from all of it. God doesn't hold us accountable for how people treat us. He does hold us accountable for how we treat and respond to them. Jesus and his forgiving power became more real to me that night.

Three hours later, I was approached as if nothing had happened. There was no anger. There was only peace and calm. I was able to smile and ask how the day had been. I never even mentioned what had happened concerning the denial of the baby. I took a bath, studied the word of God, and went to sleep. It was a peaceful sleep. I rested knowing that when it was all said and done, God would have the last word in and over my life.

I hadn't slept so peacefully in months. I felt it had to be the peace like Jesus had as he slept through the storm while with the disciples when going to the other side in the boat. In Mark 4:38-39, the word of the God says, "And he was in the hinder part of the ship, asleep on a pillow: and they awake him, and say unto him, Master, carest thou not that we perish? And he arose, and rebuked the wind, and said unto the sea, Peace, be still. And the wind ceased, and there was a great calm." I can testify that from that day forth I had a peace that wouldn't be shaken and a calm that can not be explained.

Losing my baby was very hurtful. For a long time I admit, I didn't understand it. Now, I give God all the praise. Not only was it the best thing for me, it would have been a terrible situation for a baby to be raised in. And I know I couldn't have taken my child being abused in any way.

God is so awesome that as I was writing this book, he was allowing the Holy Spirit to speak to me and heal me at the same time. Last week on my way home, the spirit of the Lord spoke to me and said, "Turn off your stereo." When I turned it off, I heard him say, "You have unforgiveness." I said out loud, "What?" He said again, "You have unforgiveness." I said, "Lord, unforgiveness about what?" He then said, "You have unforgivenness towards your ex-husband for denying your baby during your divorce and you need to confess it out loud."

As I drove down highway 495, I began to confess out loud my unforgiveness and began to cry. Only this time it wasn't a wounded cry. It was a sound I had never heard come from my body before. I began to cry out "Lord, I'm sorry. Please forgive me for my unforgiveness." He didn't stop there. He continued to tell me that I had unforgiveness towards one of my ex in-laws for mistreating me. I had unforgivenees towards my father for things I experienced during my childhood. Then he told me I had unforgiveness for myself because my baby died.

As I continued to drive, confessing my unforgiveness and crying out to God, I had a feeling of being free that I never had before in my life. I heard a Bishop say that a lot of our blessings were wrapped up in unforgiveness. I never realized that I had not forgiven these people. I sure didn't realize I had not forgiven myself. I am glad, however, that I serve a God who speaks to my heart. He cleanses me from all unrighteousness. He continues to show and reveal himself to me. He lets me know how much he loves me. I am so thankful and it makes me love him and want to serve him even more.

No matter what we go through in life and no matter who hurts us, we have to forgive. In Matthew 6:13, the word of God says, "If you forgive people their sins, your Father in heaven will forgive your sins also." Forgiveness is continual. In Matthew 18:21-22, the word of the God says, "Then came Peter to him, and said, Lord, how oft shall my brother sin against me, and I forgive him? till seven times? Jesus saith unto him, I say not unto thee, Until seven times: but, Until seventy times seven." To some this may seem like a lot times to forgive someone for mistreating and/or causing harm. In order to help accept it inside your heart, ask yourself this question: How many times has Jesus forgiven me?

As I study the word of God and come to know him more, I not only love him more, but I am thankful for his grace and his mercy. Unforgiveness sets up a root of bitterness from deep within that causes torment to the person who refuses to forgive. Unforgiveness can not only kill you, but will also cause one to be cut off from the blessings of God. And I want all that God has for me.

I thank the Lord for allowing this to be revealed to me. I thank him for giving me yet another opportunity to repent and to forgive. I'm thankful he continues to perform his plan for my life to completion in order that I might continue to grow in him as he makes me into the Woman of God he wants me to be.

Hebrews 12:14-15 reminds me to "Follow peace with all men, and holiness, without which no man shall see the Lord: Looking diligently lest any man fail of the grace of God; lest any root of bitterness springing up trouble you, and thereby many be defiled." Since Jesus has forgiven me, I can forgive others, and surely I can also forgive myself. When he forgives us and frees us, it's up to us to accept and receive it. I can sincerely say that I forgive them all.

Although I do not have any babies naturally, the Lord has blessed me to have many godchildren whom I love dearly. Some of them call me mama. The ages range from two years to 25-years-old. I call them all my babies. Being in the position like a mother, I teach them to never let anything or anyone separate them from their relationship with God. His love is real, honest, and unconditional. The love of God is not just something I've heard about. I experience his love personally every day of my life. So can you.

CHAPTER 7

What Mother's Should Teach

(In the Book of Proverbs, Chapter 31) The mother of king Lemuel taught him he was not only the son who came from her womb, or the son of her vows (her solemn promise to the responsibility bestowed her); but that he was a king. He was a man who had to be wise. He was not give himself to just any woman, or treats them any way nor behaves himself in ways that would destroy his reputation as a king.

Lemuel's mother also told him that kings do not drink wine; nor does a prince (being of or in a royal family, especially the son of a reigning king or queen) drink strong drink because it could cause one to forget the law and alter his judgment of any of the afflicted. She informs him of what kind of man he should be. He should make good decisions and judgments not only for himself, but on behalf of and towards others.

His mother speaks to him about characteristics of a virtuous woman. This was so that when he sees her, he will recognize her. Not only will he recognize her, but he will nurture, care, and support her in what God has purposed for her. He will take his rightful place as the head of the house, and she will assist him in accomplishing the vision God has given him for them, their children, and their children's children. His steps will be ordered by God, and whatsoever he will do shall prosper according to the word of God which does not return unto him void. She will respect him, and her children will rise up and call her blessed and she will show her happiness by the countenance of her face.

Her heart will be made glad, and she will have peace that passes understanding. Nothing shall be able to separate her from her first love which is Christ Jesus. He will be her King. She will be his Queen and what God has joined together let no man put asunder. They will know the true meaning of love through the love of the Lord Jesus Christ. Jesus Christ who died for you and for me that we might know who he was so that we might know who we are in and through him.

"If You Can't Tell It, Let Me Tell It!"

Of all my years of hearing sermons about Proverbs 31, never had anyone brought out that before the mention of the virtuous woman there was a mother teaching her son how to be the king of the virtuous woman. This point blew my mind because so often I've heard it said that women love their sons and raise their daughters. Therefore, the mother oftentimes creates a nightmare for the woman who marries him.

It appears that at one point in the passage, Lemuel's mother is reminding him of who he is and his demeanor and behavior should exhibit that of a King. She reminds him that he came from her womb and that she had made some vows to God concerning him. He is not to disrespect himself nor disrespect whom he represents. She teaches him from the heart of a mother by being honest with him. She is not condoning or expecting inappropriate behavior from him. She is holding him accountable, letting him know it, and teaching him what he is accountable for.

A mother who really loves her children will be honest about them and with them. A mother who really loves her children will teach them right from wrong. A mother should teach her son that he shouldn't sleep around with different women no matter how popular society says it is. A mother should teach her son that he should not have babies all over town. A mother should teach her son that he cannot be a daddy in several places at one time. A mother should teach her son that he should treat women with respect at all times. A mother should teach her son that he should not beat a woman. A mother should teach her son to admit when he is wrong and stand up for what is right. A mother should teach her son responsibility and not do everything for him. A mother should teach her son by telling him when he is wrong and not condoning him in his wrong doing. A mother should teach her son not to be abusive to himself or others. A mother should teach her son to admit the truth and not be in denial. A mother should teach her son not to marry anyone until he's ready. Marriage is serious a commitment. A mother should teach her son to live independently on his own. A mother should teach her son that a woman is not just to pleasure his physical needs. A mother should teach her son to love God first and foremost.

There are many things a woman should teach her son, especially about what his responsibility is when it comes to marrying a virtuous woman. A mother should teach her son that a man takes care of his family. A mother should teach her son that he should leave his father and mother and cleave to his wife. A mother should teach her son that if he cannot leave his father and mother, he can not truly cleave to his wife. A mother should teach her son that he has to love himself before he can love someone else. A mother should teach her son that he shouldn't treat any woman in a way he wouldn't want his mother, his grandmother, sisters, nieces, or his daughters to be treated. Proverbs 31 begins with the conversation of a mother teaching her son. It is awesome and mothers should take note.

My experience has taught me that all women who give birth are not mothers. I thank God for those of you who are, those of you who were, and those who will become mothers. May God bless all mothers in the future to teach your sons that they are kings and should behave and conduct themselves as such. May God bless you to teach them according to the word of God and may you be the virtuous women of God whose children will call you blessed in the name of Jesus Christ.

This chapter of God's word is personal because not only had it not been revealed to me like this before, but I had not noticed the King's name being Lemuel. See, my grandfather's (my mother's father) name was Lemuel. This touched the core of my spirit because I now know that should God desire me to have any male in my life, he should not only present himself as a king, but he will have been taught how to treat me as his queen by his mother. His mother would also be a virtuous woman of God.

I always deserved a king. I always have. I just didn't realize it. Proverbs 31 is personal and dear to my heart. I will never look at it the same again. Since my past choices have not been kings, I've decided not to choose. I have a lot of choices and have made this decision. Should God choose to bless me with a king; he will be God's choice. Should he not, I'm happy with the King of Kings. This Chapter is dedicated to the grandfather I never knew, Mr. "Lemuel" Cline. May your soul now rest in peace.

CHAPTER 8

Many Choices, One Decision

(**I**n the Book of Esther, Chapter 5**)** There was a king by the name of Ahasuerus who sat on the throne of his kingdom, which was in Shushan the palace. In the third year of his reign; he had a feast for all his princes and his servants. After days of showing off his riches, he had a feast for all the people who were present in Shushan the palace which was decorated beautifully. Vashti, the queen at the time, also had a feast for the women in the royal house which belonged to king Ahasuerus. On the seventh day, when the king was drunk with wine, he commanded the seven chamberlains that served him to bring Vashti before the king with the crown royal. He wanted to show the people and the princes how pretty she was. The queen Vashti refused to come at the king's commandment, and the king became angry and embarrassed. Yet, she would not obey him.

Then the king asked the wise men, which knew the laws at the time, what he should do with the Queen since she disobeyed him. One of them, by the name of Memucan, told the king that Vashti had not only wronged the king, but also all the princes, and all the people. Therefore, she should be an example to all women who disobey their husbands. They wanted it to be made known that her title and royal estate would be given to someone who was better than she was.

The King was to make a decree that shall be published throughout all his empire. All wives were to give to their husbands honor no matter what they thought about it. This pleased the king and the princes; and the king did according to what Memucan recommended.

He sent letters to all the people in every language that every man should rule in his house. After the king was satisfied with the new decree, he remembered what Vashti had done. His servants ministered to him and said, "Let there be fair young virgins sought for the king." Officers were appointed to gather together all the fair young virgins to Shushan the palace. The house of the women who were the keepers of the women made sure they were purified. This meant whomever the king wanted would be queen instead of Vashti.

In the palace there was a Jew by the name of Mordecai, who was a Benjamite. He brought up Hadassah, Esther, his uncle's daughter who was fair and beautiful. Mordecai raised her as his daughter after her parents had died. When the king's commandment and his decree were heard, maidens gathered together at the Shushan palace in the custody of Hegai. She was the keeper of women. Esther was also brought to the king's house. She pleased him, and obtained his kindness. He quickly gave her things for purification. He also gave her seven maidens out of the king's house. Esther and her maids were given the best place in the house.

Esther had not told anyone who she was or who she was related to at the advice of Mordecai. He walked by the court of the women's house every day to check and see how Esther was doing. This happened for twelve months, according to the way things were done back then. There was six months for their purification to be completed with six months with oil of myrrh and six months with sweet scents and other things for purifying them. After this the maidens came to the king and were given whatever they wanted. She was then returned to a second house of women where she was given to the custody of Shaashgaz, the king's chamberlain, who kept the concubines. She was no longer obligated to come to the king, but since he liked her, he called her by her name.

When Esther went to the king, she didn't ask for anything except what the king's keeper of women had appointed to her. This made her obtain favor with the king, so she remained in his house, and the king loved Esther more than all the other women. Since he favored her more than any of the virgins, he made her queen instead of Vashti. The king had another feast with all the princes and his servants. When the virgins were gathered the second time, Mordecai sat in the king's gate with two of the king's chamberlains who watched the door.

After Esther was queen, there was a promotion given to Haman the son of Hammedatha. He was promoted to be above all the princes that were with him and the king's servants bowed and reverenced him because the king commanded it. But Mordecai would not bow nor give reverence to him. The king's servants noticed it and asked why he didn't obey the king's commandment daily. Mordecai ignored them so they told Haman because they thought it would make Mordecai bow to him since he had told them he was a Jew. Haman hated the Jews so when he noticed that

Mordecai would not bow or reverence him, he became angry and set out to kill him.

Haman told the king that there were people who were not keeping his laws and that he should write a decree to have them destroyed. Haman even offered to pay the people who would take care of destroying the people who wouldn't obey the king's laws. The king took his ring from his hand and gave it to Haman as an agreement between them. Haman was then given charge over the people to do whatever he deemed appropriate. The decree was written and the agreement between the two was sealed with the king's ring.

The letters were sent to destroy and kill all Jews, both young and old, little children and women, in one day, which was the thirteenth day of the twelfth month. When Mordecai found out about it he was so upset that he tore his clothes, put on sackcloth with ashes, and went to the city and cried. One of Esther's maids told her what had happened. She sent someone to put clothes on Mordecai and take him away, but he would not listen. Esther called one of the king's chamberlains who had been appointed to her to find out from Mordecai why he was so upset.

Hatach went to Mordecai and Mordecai told him what had happened and about the sum of money promised to the king's treasuries for the Jews to be destroyed. He gave a copy of the decree to Hatach to show Esther. He wanted her to go to the king and request he change the decree on behalf of her people. Hatach came and told Esther what Mordecai had said. Esther was afraid because she knew the law was to put to death anyone who entered the inner court without being called by the king. It didn't matter if they were man or woman, the person would be killed unless the king was holding out the golden scepter. Esther had not been called to the king in thirty days and was afraid.

Mordecai sent word to Esther asking her if she thought she would not be killed just because she was in his house. He reminded her that she too was a Jew. He told her she could not be silent and hold her peace when she had the opportunity to help deliver her people. Mordecai asked Esther how she knew that this was not the reason she had been placed there at this time. With that question, Esther sent word to Mordecai to get all the Jews together. She requested for them to fast for three days and nights. She and her maidens were also going to fast. She would go before the king in spite of the law. She said, "And if I perish, I perish."

Mordecai did what Esther told him and Esther put on her royal apparel and stood in the inner court where the king could see her. When he saw her, again she obtained his favor. He held out the golden scepter in his hand. When Esther touched the scepter, the king asked her what her request was and he granted it.

"If You Can't Tell It, Let Me Tell It!"

When I think back about some of the opportunities I've been given in life, I must admit I didn't take advantage of all of them. Nor when I was in a backslidden situation did I think anything good could come out of it. When I repented and made the commitment to give my life totally for the Lord, it was the beginning of test after test. This test resulted in my having several choices. The choices were not the problem. Making the decision was.

It is not an easy decision to put myself out for the entire world. There are many things that come into question. How will it affect your life after the news is out about this book? Will it affect your work on a professional level? Many times different scenarios came to mind. Then I thought of my nieces, my goddaughters, my cousins, my friend's children, and all the women like me who know that someone has to tell their stories. I had a choice to tell my story and let someone else write it. I had a choice to write under a pen name and no one would know who I was. I had a lot of choices and made a decision.

The decision was people needed to know that this happened to a real person. This is not fiction or some character made up by someone with an awesome imagination. This is real and God is real. This is not what I've heard. This is what I experienced and lived through with the help of the Lord. These are things he brought me through in my life. I have to tell of his goodness.

When I committed my life to Christ, my life no longer belonged to me and I told him he could do with me what he pleased. He put this book in my spirit to write and he told me how to write it. My choice is to be obedient. My decision is to tell it. I am not saying that this book will help everybody, but it is dedicated to every woman. If this book helps one person, then my suffering has not been in vain. Of all the choices I had, I chose to tell it.

From these experiences, I too have been at the point like Esther where I felt that if "I perish, I perish." I often sought advice from a female friend who knew the state laws. We became friends and I shared some things with her about my relationship. Mostly we talked about how I felt about losing my baby and how abusive the relationship was. She would invite me to her house, just to visit, watch football games, and attend family functions just to get out and be around people. After being invited to attend a football game, I thought maybe doing activities with other couples might be helpful, so we accepted the invitation.

After a while, it didn't take a genius to figure out that the relationship wasn't the best one. Needless to say, there was no conversation all the way to the house. That was pretty normal, so it didn't seem odd to me. I was becoming numb to the events taking place in the relationship. The cursing, accusations, and name calling didn't offend or hurt me any more.

Later that night, I was called by that same friend checking on my physical safety. It was felt that I shouldn't have told anyone anything about what I was going through or how I was feeling about it. With a concerned voice, she communicated to me that it was said that if I thought about doing anything to cause this person any pain that my legs would be cut off from under me. Yes, it was a threat in my opinion, and a very serious one. Only this time, I didn't care. I had gotten to the point where the threats didn't scare me. They only made me plan to get away from the bondage of abuse and lies I lived for the past year and a half.

I told her that I was fine and was going to bed. She told me that she would remain alert and offered me a place to stay if I needed one. The next day I began doing research via the computer regarding domestic violence, looking for women's shelters and began documenting his actions. All I knew was that should something happen to me, I was not going to be another body found and leave my family wondering what happened. Had he done anything to me, I was going to make sure the police would know who to look for first. All I could do was pray and trust God who said he'd never leave or forsake me.

That night, my mind was full of thoughts on my way to church. I was wondering, "What should I do now? Should I go back to Texas?" There was one point in my life when I was in fear and I didn't feel safe. But that night at church, something happened to me that I will never forget. I started crying and couldn't stop. One of the Minister's wives came and hugged me. All of a sudden, I heard the voice of the Pastor's wife, Sister Wanda Roberts, saying, "Oh God. Sister Arnold, I don't know what it is, but just say thank you Jesus." I began to say it although I didn't feel like what I was going through was something to thank him for. I thanked him out of obedience. I thanked him because the pain was so severe. I was willing to do anything to ease or stop it. I started saying "Thank you

Jesus" over and over again. Sister Wanda's words stayed in my mind, "Just say thank you Jesus," and that is what I did.

Eventually, I stopped worrying about anyone or anything around me. I was just thanking Jesus through every thought, through every pain. I felt my body shaking and I could hear myself but I couldn't stop thanking him. All of a sudden it was like the Holy Spirit himself stood up in me. Immediately, I stopped crying and straightened myself up. Strength entered my body that I never felt before. I felt the power of the Holy Spirit in me and around me. It wasn't only a physical strength; it was strength deep in the soul of my being.

As I stood up, I walked down the aisle toward the Pastor. Elder Dr. Sherman L. Roberts, said, "Sister Arnold, you just got your breakthrough. God said you don't have to cry any more." Sister Robert's and some of the other members were praising God. I remember walking but not saying anything. In my mind I was thinking, "Is that all you've got devil? If that's all you've got, you're going to have to come with something better than that to take me out." Things were different for me from that night on. I was ready to fight. And this fight wasn't only regarding my physical health. This was a fight for my soul.

After service was over, Sister Wanda hugged me, looked at me, and smiled. She said, "Sister Arnold, you had your hands on your hips and it reminded me of the old mothers in the church who would walk around the church with their hands on their hips when they had prayed to God and he had finally given them an answer." I just smiled. I didn't know exactly what had happened. All I knew was, I wasn't the same. I was ready to stop crying and see God do what his word said he would do. I was no longer willing to settle any more for anything less than what God said I could have. I wasn't going to be less than who he predestined me to be. I was ready to stand up for God at all cost no matter what or who I had to stand up to.

I returned to the house and must have looked different because no one said a word to me. I didn't get cursed out and there was complete silence. About two hours later, I heard something being said to me. I didn't understand what it was since I was still somewhat out of it due to my "Breakthrough."

Before I lay down, I began to pray. After I finished praying, I got into bed. A few minutes later I got out of bed and went to see what was said that I didn't hear. I wanted to know if there was something we suddenly needed to talk about since I only heard mumbling. I asked what had been said to me. I was looked at with a smirk. Then I was told with a smile that I had no idea what was about to happen to me. As I stood in the doorway I said, "You know what? I'm not afraid of you. I don't care what you think you can do to me because everything you try to do to me or think you've done to me is going to be turned around on you and your family. So, do what you think you need to do. God is going to take care of me. He always has and always will." I turned around, walked away, and went to bed.

Later, I talked with one of my friends. We laughed as I told her, I had a "Color Purple" moment. As a matter of fact, I didn't think I could be hurt any more than I already had. Even if the plan was to kill me, as Paul said, "Absent in the body, present with the Lord." I was tired of the situation. Whatever God had decided was fine with me. I had made my peace with God. That is all that mattered to me. I felt like it was okay that my body had gone through hell. As long as when I died, my soul did not go to hell, I was fine. I had a many choices, but I made one decision. My decision was to stay with God fearful and all.

Since I had prayed and trusted God would do what he said he would do, he touched me in a way he never had before. I was reminded of a passage in Daniel 10:7-12, where the word of God says, "And I Daniel alone saw the vision: for the men that were with me saw not the vision; but a great quaking fell upon them, so that they fled to hide themselves. Therefore I was left alone, and saw this great vision, and there remained no strength in me: for my comeliness was turned in me into corruption, and I retained no strength. Yet heard I the voice of his words: and when I heard the voice of his words, when was I in a deep sleep on my face, and my face toward the ground. And, behold, a hand touched me, which set me upon my knees and upon the palms of my hands. And he said unto me, O Daniel, a man greatly beloved, understand the words that I speak unto thee, and stand upright: for unto thee am I now sent. And when he had spoken this word unto me, I stood trembling. Then said he unto me, Fear not, Daniel: for from the first day that thou didst set thine heart to understand and to chasten thyself before thy God, thy words were heard, and I am come for thy words."

I have no doubt that God heard my prayers and the prayers of the righteous who were praying with me and for me that night at Full Gospel Church of God by Faith. I am thankful to God he placed me at Full Gospel Church of God by Faith. The Pastor is Elder Dr. Sherman L. Roberts and Sister Wanda Roberts is the first lady. I am thankful most of all to God who not only hears me when I pray, but he allows me to hear him when he speaks. Speak Lord, that your children may hear from you as we continue to do your will and go through in order to get to where you have called us to be in Jesus name. Selah.

CHAPTER 9

Going Through To Get To

(In the Book of Ruth, Chapter 1) There was a man in the time when judges ruled by the name of Elimelech. His wife was Naomi and they had two sons, Mahlon and Chilion. When they came to Moab, Elimelech had died. After their father died, Mahlon and Chilion married Orpah and Ruth. They were together about ten years. Mahlon and Chilion also died and Naomi told her daughters-in-laws that she might leave because she heard in the country of Moab how the Lord was providing for his people. She decided to leave with her two daughters-in-laws and returned to Judah.

At that point, Naomi told her daughters-in-laws for each one of them to return to their mother's house. She blessed them and prayed that the Lord deal kindly with them, that the Lord grants them rest and for them to have another husband. She kissed them and cried. They questioned if they should return to their families and she asked them why should they go with her. She had no more sons for them to marry. She wanted them to have the opportunity to be married and be happy with their husbands. Orpah decided to leave, Ruth refused to leave. She told Naomi she would not leave her and where ever she went, Ruth said she would go with her. She told Naomi when you die, I will die and where you are buried, I will be also.

Naomi saw that Ruth was serious, so they went to Bethlehem. When they arrived, someone in the city recognized Naomi; but she told them to call her Mara because she felt the Lord had dealt bitterly with her. She felt as though she left with everything and came back with nothing. Ruth eventually married Boaz.

"If You Can't Tell It, Let Me Tell It!"

This is a very unique story in the bible about a daughter-in-law who chose to stay with her mother in-law instead of returning home. There aren't many women that I know of who would be willing to stay with their in-laws. But I remember how my grandmother (my daddy's mother) was towards her in-laws, particularly my mother. I can remember her hearing rumors about her children behaving inappropriately and she would come to town with a vengeance. Although they were her children, she didn't allow them to abuse anyone else's child. She knew it wasn't right and she knew they weren't raised to mistreat people.

I do understand that dealing with in-laws on any level can be trying. I remember going to visit an in-law once who had clearly let me know she loved her brother so much, she wished they didn't have any other siblings. At first, I thought they were just that close and didn't take it too seriously. I should have. I knew when she called, she wouldn't speak. She would just ask for her brother. If I said he wasn't home, she would say, "Tell him I called" and would hang up. Finally, it got to a point when I would interrupt her and said, "How are you?" She would answer, "fine" and continue as usual.

The time came when I had the pleasure of meeting her. After arriving at her house for maybe five minutes and meeting her in person for the first time, she said, "Oh, I made arrangements for you to stay with the neighbors." I said, "Excuse me." She then repeated her comments again. She was then informed that before there would be a separation of overnight arrangements, we would be staying at a hotel.

Since that wasn't an option for her brother who told her the arrangements were unacceptable, she miraculously found room for us to stay in the same house. Today, it is funny. At the time, I remember being so offended I thought to myself, "And when you come to visit, I will make arrangements for you to sleep outside with the dog." Thank God for forgiveness and deliverance.

I don't know of many in-laws who would want their daughter in-laws to stay with them. The times I remember when there was an opportunity for an in-law to have a positive influence on me never happened. There was a time when I was talking to in-laws about the abusive language and treatment I received. I was told to turn a deaf ear and ignore it. I guess this was how they had handled things being done to them over the years. I remember thinking, "I'm not you and that is ridiculous."

After the miscarriage, I thought I could find comfort from an in-law. I has just spoken to my mother and told her about losing the baby. We both were upset since I'm the only one who doesn't have children. I hung up the phone and went to an in-law for comfort. When I was asked why

I was crying, I explained I was sad about losing my baby, how I had just told my mother, who was now also upset. I will never forget the words or the tone in which the words were spoken to me. "Apparently, it wasn't meant to be, so you might as well get over it." I felt like I had just been hit in the stomach and my tears instantly stopped. I couldn't believe a person could be so cruel. I had never known anyone to be so cruel or say such a cruel thing to a person before. There was no compassion or empathy at all. But I learned another lesson. When people show you who they are, believe them.

Another night, I was told about a get together to watch a football game. Supposedly there were no women attending, so I wasn't invited. However, after a visit from a friend who asked why I wasn't coming to the party, I called and questioned why I had been lied to. An argument started on the phone which ended with me being hung up on. Shortly afterwards, I began having chest pains and drove myself to the hospital. It was about an hour later when one of the in-laws showed up, but never asked how I felt after returning to the house that night.

About 30 minutes to an hour after returning from the ER, I was in bed resting, I heard footsteps. My door swung open and the cursing and yelling started. As I was trying to explain I had just returned from the Emergency Room, I was being threatened and told to get out of the house. With only inches to move, I was able to dial 911. After the family members heard what was going on, they entered the room. The only thing said was, "Whatever you do, just don't hit her."

Again, the police made no arrest and there were no words of comfort or support. There was no conversation about inappropriate behavior or disrespect. The next day, one of the relatives left to return home and it was as though nothing had taken place in that house. There were no questions of concern regarding how I felt. Nothing was said; not one word.

A few days later, I had to wear a heart monitor for 24 hours and more tests were taken the next month. The chest pains were stress related and nothing ever showed up on the test results. It's amazing how much better I felt once I left not only the drama of the relationship, but the drama of the entire household. At first it was hard for me to understand how I could end up in a relationship with someone who could be so different from whom they portrayed themselves to be.

Then, I remembered a conversation I had with one of the relatives who said, "Never show a person who you really are because they can use it against you." As I looked at her I thought, "You don't even know who you are. Who is it that I've been talking to? Who is it that I met?" It was like a light bulb went off in my head. I remember hearing that a child's behavior shouldn't be considered strange. Look at the concept that children are a product of their parents. I finally began to understand why the relationship had been crazy. That was a crazy way to live your life every day.

Now that I am out of the situation, I've had time to think back to the day in which the contractual agreement took place. I remember having a conversation with two of the other in-laws who welcomed me to the family with little or no enthusiasm. Later, I remembered attending the wedding of one of the relatives. As I looked around the table, I noticed all the siblings were socializing while their spouses were sitting at the table not talking. As I looked into the faces of each one of them, I realized they all looked as miserable as I looked. Even more interesting was no one introduced us to each other. The atmosphere proved interesting to say the least. I later found that in this family in-laws aren't considered family. In-laws were considered relatives by marriage only. That was a new one on me.

Mother's and/or Father-in-laws should also understand that he or she is only the mother/father when it comes to their children's marital relationship. They are not their son's or daughter's companion, lover, girlfriend or boyfriend, wife nor husband. A mother is the mother. Only when a mother/father can honestly and truly understand this will the in-law relationship flourish. A mother/father who doesn't understand his/her role after the son/daughter is married can be as poisonous to a relationship as the most venomous snake. This also causes the couple and their children to stay away. Sometimes they even move to another state all together. They only visit for short periods of time. They don't even send the grandchildren for summer visits. So, if you're a mother/father and you identify with some of these issues, you might want to reevaluate some things you're doing or have done in the lives of your children and their spouses.

It's often said we go through things in life to help us grow, become stronger, and learn what life is all about. I can honestly say for someone my age, I've experienced a lot. So much to the point where I once told my mother of an experience I had in college. She said, "I am an adult and I don't ever want to have to experience anything like that."(But that's another book). The in-law experiences I've had has taught me a lot. Should I ever be blessed to be a mother in-law or any type of relative by marriage, I will know how not to treat them.

I would rather follow the example of after my grandmother when it comes to being an in-law. Her name was Lucy Bradshaw. I remember although my aunts and uncles were adults with families, if she heard of them not behaving in a respectful manner towards anyone, especially their spouses or children, everyone would be paid a visit.

One time, I remember my dad and his siblings were all gathered at my aunt's house. I remember them arguing trying to figure out who had done something wrong that caused her to be on her way to see them. If there was an in-law that she didn't like, I don't know who it could have been. All I ever saw her do was show love and respect for all of them. I've never heard one in-law speak anything other than words about her kindness shown towards them.

One of the most awesome qualities I remember about my grandmother is that she didn't care if you were her child or not, if you were wrong you were wrong. She did not condone your wrong no matter if it was in public or behind closed doors. She would tell you just what she thought and didn't care if you liked it or not. She would admit when she was wrong, take responsibility for it, and move right along. She expected her children and her grandchildren to do the same thing when it came to taking responsibility for their actions. And she meant for all of us to do exactly what we said we would do. No foolishness was accepted, and everyone knew it.

Mammaw had this rule. We had to spend the 4th of July at her house. She didn't care if you came to visit her for any other holiday except the 4th of July. I often wondered why the 4th of July was such an important holiday to her. I remember a story she shared with me once. She said, "When I was about three years old, I saw my grandmother sold on a slave block." She seemed so sad. I never questioned her about it and I never heard my dad or his siblings mention it.

All I know is her independence meant a lot to her and she let it be known. It didn't matter who you were, it didn't matter how far away you lived, nor did it matter who you were married to. You were expected to be at her house on July 4th. No exceptions were given to anyone. And no excuse was a good enough reason for not showing up. I loved that about her. She was consistent and you knew where you stood with her. If you didn't know, she had no problem letting you know.

I loved our family being together at her house. All the kids played while the adults cooked. This was the time they had their bonding moment.

It was strange how after mammaw died, the entire family structure seemed to fall apart. It kind of reminds me of the movie Soul Food.

When Mammaw died, the 4th of July family gathering stopped. At her funeral the in-laws appeared to be just as upset as her biological children. I am thankful to God that he blessed me to be around her as long as I was. I not only think of her often, but I really miss her. This chapter is dedicated to my grandmother, Lucy Bradshaw. May you rest in peace.

CHAPTER 10

Woman Of God, You Are

One Sunday night, I was invited to a women's program at a church called the House of Prayer. One of the speakers was Missionary Helen Tate. Her topic was "When Weeping Women Pray, They Give Birth To A Blessing." She started by saying, "One of the most difficult challenges facing our society today is the struggle to know who we are as a people. There is an identity crisis among society and people are trying so desperately to become something in life. People try to fit in to a particular group, wasting precious time, money and energy to be something they're not instead of being who they really are. We, as a people of God, need to seek God, our creator, and allow him to reveal who we really are to us."

Missionary Tate went on to ask if anyone had heard the saying "I am what God says I am, and I can do what God says I can do?" I am not sure who came up with the saying, but I'm sure we've all heard it from time to time. Unfortunately, as she said, most of us did not hear about it during our childhood. The most things spoken in my life by people were about what I would not be and what I could not do. Currently, as an adult, it is as though I had to be deprogrammed from what people have imparted into my mind and allow God to reprogram into me what he says I can be through his word.

Awe-inspiring, Missionary Tate spoke about women giving birth from a spiritual perspective. Missionary Tate said, "Every woman should be pregnant with something. Every woman should know what it's like to travail in labor. Whatever a woman births becomes a blessing. However, her blessing is not a blessing unless it is shared. The women in the bible were blessed to be a blessing."

She went on to say, "Some women are on Spiritual Birth Control. Some women are spiritual abortionist. Some women carry a still birth blessing that lies dormant and lifeless. And some women deliver prematurely."

Missionary Tate expounded on the word of God that night from a viewpoint in which all women can relate.

For some time now, I've tried to put into words what I felt God had imparted into my spirit as a woman who once visited the well. That night I heard the explanation put in powerful anointed words spoken by Missionary Helen Tate who concluded with this poem called "Woman of God, You Are. As she gave birth to the words of the poem, I was so blessed by them. I pray that you are blessed by them as well.

Woman of God, You Are
By: Helen Tate

Woman of God, You are:	More than a label given by society as a sex symbol.
Woman of God, You are:	More than the reason for a man's erection.
Woman of God, You are:	You are a power container mighty and powerful in the Spirit.
Woman of God, You are:	One who has been given the ability to travail in the Spirit.
Woman of God, You are:	A Birther, who brings forth life.
Woman of God, You are:	Multi-tasking who does many things at the same time.
Woman of God, You are:	A Producer who brings forth, brings about, and causes to exist or rise.
Woman of God, You are:	A Multiplier who whatever you touch, you cause to increase.
Woman of God, You are:	A Seer who is able to visualize, predict and assist in development.
Woman of God, You are:	A Developer who has the power to sway and produce effects.
Woman of God, You are:	A Caregiver who brings comfort to those around you and in your care.
Woman of God, You are:	Blessed to be a blessing.
Woman of God, You are:	Who the word of God predestined you to be.
Woman of God, You are:	What the word of God ordained you to be.
Woman of God, You are:	A Woman of God

Missionary Helen Tate is the President and founder of Victory In Praise Printing, in Amityville, New York.

I have been blessed by another woman of God in my life. I've seen her go through so much yet, her faith was stronger than mine. She is a woman of God whom I saw raise a son whose father never saw him until he was two-years-old. Yet, she allowed the father to pursue a relationship with him. I saw a woman of God struggle to ensure her son never did without.

She is a woman of God I remember running in the rain with her son to secure an apartment because she couldn't get a ride to the complex from family members. She is a woman of God I remember having the faith to say, "I am going to work for this company" and refused to take anything else until it came to fruition.

She is a woman of God who is gifted and talented in many ways. She can create floral masterpieces, decorate a house for the fraction of the cost, connect you with the resources you never knew existed, has every user friendly gadget to ensure your home runs smoothly, has a heart of gold, and has not yet began to see the blessing that God has in store for her.

She is a woman of God who has cried with me and for me as I would go through my struggles. She is a woman of God who sacrificed her body by carrying my couch on her back when I had to move in the winter to my first apartment. She is a woman who protected me when we were growing up.

She is a woman of God who makes me smile when she reminds me of the story of her saving my life because I refused to walk. My mother was tired of carrying me so she put me down and said, "You either walk or stay here" and kept walking. Not knowing that my mother wouldn't really leave me, (I don't think), this woman of God, being a child herself at the time, came back to get me.

I remember so many wonderful things about you that touched my heart. You have no idea what a powerful woman of God you are. This woman of God is the mother of Christopher A. Norton, (Auntie D's Snookems) and the grandmother of (Miss CeCe-Boom) Ci'Ara Norton. This chapter is dedicated to a woman of God that I love beyond words. May God bless you Woman of God. This chapter is dedicated to you, my sister, Barbara M. Whitmore.

CHAPTER 11

The Fellowship Of His Suffering

(**I**n **the book of Philippians, Chapter 3**) the word of God says, "That I may know him, and the power of his resurrection, and the fellowship of his sufferings, being made conformable unto his death; If by any means I might attain unto the resurrection of the dead."

People have always talked about the power of the resurrection of Jesus. Some speak of him getting up with all power in his hands. Many talk, about the blessings and what he is able to bless us with, and I've heard it said that he's a lawyer in a court room and doctor in a sick room. He's a wheel in the middle of the wheel and many more positive, nice convenient, happy feelings and sayings. And I do not demean or disgrace his resurrection at all.

But, from what I've learned, a real child of God knows the fellowship of his sufferings. It's a daily journey we must take. It's the cup we must endure. It's the time when we have the "Nevertheless" moments like Jesus did in the garden. We pray and ask for God to move on our behalf, only to say, "Your Will, Not My Will Be Done."

I just found it interesting that very seldom does anyone discuss or share how they want to experience the fellowship of his sufferings. His suffering is what makes his resurrection so powerful. Since I have been in New York, I have become familiar with the fellowship of his sufferings on more than one occasion. And in my suffering is where I came to know him and truly believe in the power of his resurrection. That is the only thing that kept me hanging on sometimes. I would say, "Yes, I'm down right now and it looks real bad like I'm not going to make it. Whatever I went through, I know Jesus had to suffer and die, but he did rise again. And I knew that I too would rise again." No matter what the situation is you go through, God can turn your story around for his Glory.

By now, you've probably had a few memories surface. You may have even felt some pain and/or hurts from your past surface as you read. Have you given yourself time to think about it? Maybe deep down inside, you feel like you can't tell it. Maybe you still aren't ready to tell it. Ask yourself this question? Why not? Now let me ask you some questions? When you think about the memories of your past, does it still cause you to become angry? Does it still cause you pain? Does it bring negative thoughts to mind?   Are you thinking to yourself that it doesn't matter anymore? It's in the past, right? You've moved on, right? What difference does it make, right? I'm over it, right? Ask yourself this question: If it doesn't matter, *why can't you tell it?*

CHAPTER 12

New Beginnings, Let Me Tell It

In case you were wondering, I do have an ending to this story. This is my testimony of the beginning of what God is doing for me. Let me tell it like this.

1. Before I had to move or be put on the street, God blessed me with a job working for the State of New York with an incredible supervisor and her staff.
2. The department I work in has a bereavement program and I was able to grieve, heal, and finally write the name "Baby Arnold" under deaths in my Bible.
3. Since it was a State position, I didn't get paid for one month. I had $23.00 to last me before I received my first check. I sowed a faith seed at my church and at that very moment, God touched the hearts of people. By the time I returned to the house, there was over $80.00 in my purse.
4. The day after my divorce papers were signed, God touched the hearts of seven people who wired money to my account so I would have enough money to move to an apartment.
5. The couple who rented me the apartment not only helped me move in, but gave me a computer desk, a canister set, decorated the bathroom, and gave me the dining room set.
6. An ex-coworker said she was only at the job long enough for God to allow us to meet. She helped clean my apartment before I moved in and bought me my first supplies.
7. The same ex-coworker took me shopping in her jeep and when I was ready to pay for my purchases, she told me my money was no good when I was with her.
8. I planned to purchase blankets and other items for the apartment when another co-worker asked me if I could use some towels, blankets, and sheets. She had them in her car that same day.

9. I called to buy out the lease on my 2001, IS 300 Lexus and was sold the car for less than the rest of the lease with no penalties for breaking the lease.

10. The banking institution also sent me a separate check to pay the sales taxes for the vehicle.

11. My parent finally came to visit me in New York. It was for my ordination service into the Ministry on May 30, 2004 as an Evangelist. It was Pentecost Sunday.

12. A woman of God from my church and her family gave me two boxes of groceries when I first moved into my apartment.

13. The Lord blessed me to live in a nice apartment that has windows and is located on the ground level.

14. The Lord blessed me with landlords who took care of me when I was sick.

15. The Lord has given me the vision to write a series of books from this book called:

"If You Can't Tell It, Let Me Tell It! *"Testimonies of A Woman of God"*

"If You Can't Tell It, Let Me Tell It! *"Testimonies of A Man of God"*

"If You Can't Tell It, Let Me Tell It! *"Testimonies of A Wife in Ministry"*

"If You Can't Tell It, Let Me Tell It! *"Testimonies of A Single Mother"*

"If You Can't Tell It, Let Me Tell It! *"Testimonies of A Single Woman"*

"If You Can't Tell It, Let Me Tell It! *"Testimonies of A Teenager"*

16. I was moving February 15, 2004, but the Lord made it possible for me to move February 8, 2004.

17. This is number seventeen. One plus seven equals eight. Let me just say to you that the number eight in the bible means New Beginnings. This is a New Beginning for me and I just had to tell it.

CONCLUSION

To women all over the world who feel that you are down and can't go down any further than you are or have been, trust God and know that just as Jesus did, you will rise again. There was a time when I asked the Lord why this was happening to me? I stopped asking why, and said, "It's me, Lord. I am standing on your word and trusting in you. I know you are processing me for progress." I know you're going to bless me no matter what it looks like, no matter what it sounds like, and no matter what it feels like. I am standing even if I have to stand alone.

Some people may have even thought that I was down for the count. When Jesus was crucified, they thought that too. They didn't know God's plan for his life and no one knows what God's plan is for your life or mine. Had they known, they would not have treated us the way they have. They didn't know God would get the Glory in the end. I'm reminded of 1 Corinthians 2:8-10, the word of God says, "Which none of the princes of this world knew: for had they known it, they would not have crucified the Lord of glory. But as it is written, Eye hath not seen, nor ear heard, neither have entered into the heart of man, the things which God hath prepared for them that love him. But God hath revealed them unto us by his Spirit: for the Spirit searcheth all things, yea, the deep things of God." Praise the Lord.

These are just a few of my stories, but all of them end in God getting the glory. God is yet blessing and maturing me. My mother always said, "For every story you tell, there's always one so devastating, you can't tell." I know that I can't tell it all in this book, but as long as I have breath in my body, I will keep trying to. In Isaiah 43:9-11, the word of God says, "Let all the nations be gathered together, and let the people be assembled: who among them can declare this, and shew us former things? Let them bring forth their witnesses, that they may be justified: or let them hear, and say, it is truth. Ye are my witnesses, saith the Lord, and my servant whom I have chosen: that ye may know and believe me, and understand that I am he: before me there was no God formed, neither shall there be after me. I, even I, am the Lord; and beside me there is no saviour."

In all I've gone through, I am still standing, and I am still smiling. I know through all these things, I am more than a conqueror, through Christ who loves me. In the book of Romans 8:38-39, the word of the Lord says, "For I am persuaded, that neither death, nor life, nor angels, nor principalities, nor powers, nor things present, nor things to come, Nor height, nor depth, nor any other creature, shall be able to separate us from the love of God, which is in Christ Jesus our Lord."

I, Evangelist Devetta Joyce Arnold unequivocally declare, "That I am not ashamed of the Gospel of Jesus Christ, and *If You Can't Tell It, Let Me Tell It! "To God be the Glory for MY Story."*

www.ingramcontent.com/pod-product-compliance
Lightning Source LLC
Chambersburg PA
CBHW020345290526
45785CB00005B/2162

9 781418 479725